HARDPRESS.NET
HOME OF HARD-TO-FIND BOOKS

Rational Recreations
by William Hooper (M.D.)

Address:
HardPress
8345 NW 66TH ST #2561
MIAMI FL 33166-2626
USA
Email: info@hardpress.net

RATIONAL

RECREATIONS.

VOLUME THE THIRD.

CONTAINING

ELECTRICAL and MAGNETICAL

EXPERIMENTS.

RATIONAL RECREATIONS,

In which the PRINCIPLES of

NUMBERS

AND

NATURAL PHILOSOPHY

Are clearly and copiously elucidated,

BY A SERIES OF

EASY, ENTERTAINING, INTERESTING

EXPERIMENTS.

Among which are

All those commonly performed with the CARDS.

By W. HOOPER, M. D.

VOL. III.

LONDON,

Printed for L. DAVIS, Holborn ; J. ROBSON, New Bond-street;
B. LAW, Avemary-lane; and G. ROBINSON, Pater-noster-row.
MDCCLXXIV.

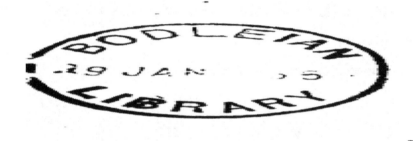

DESCRIPTION of the PLATES.

PLATE I. p. 16.

THE electric machine. The two boards *a, a,* are equal and parallel : the uppermoft has a groove, in which one of the pillars is moveable ; the other, *d,* is fixed. The brafs arm *c* fupports the axis *d* that is fixed in the globe ; *f* is the rubber, fupported by an axis in the wooden circle *g* ; *b* is a fteel fpring, regulated by a fcrew *i* ; *k* is the prime conductor, confifting of a hollow veffel of polifhed copper, and receives its electricity by means of pointed wires *m,* and the arched brafs rod *l.* The globe is turned by the wheel fixed in the moveable frame *e.* The chain *n* connects the rubber with the floor, when pofitive electricity is required.

PLATE II. p. 24.

The fquare figure *b* reprefents a plated coat of glafs. *c, d, e, f, g, b, i, j, k,* are feveral forts of jars. On the ftand, near *c,* are placed on a

VOL. III.   a   glafs

glafs the cork-balls, that ferve as an electrometer. From the end of the conductor, at *l,* hang
the bells and knobs of brafs, for the magic dance ;
s is a metal rod for taking fparks from the conductor.

P L A T E   III.   p. 104.

Fig. 1, reprefents the row of tin-foil for exhi-
biting the luminous characters.

Fig. 2. The electrical battery, confifting of
fixty-four glafs jars, which are connected by brafs
rods, that run through wires in each of them, and
the rods are connected by a chain laid over them.

P L A T E   IV.   p. 90.

Fig. 1. The electrometer. A is a light rod
that turns on the center of the femicircle B, and
has at its extremity a cork-ball C ; D is the pillar that fupports the rod.

Fig. 2. The fulmineous conductor : *a* is an
oblong pole, *b* a copper veffel in form of a funnel,
c a flender rod, terminated with a pointed wire ;
d is a wire that defcends at a foot diftance from
the building, and is carried into the room where
the experiments are to be performed.

Fig. 3. The electric branch and table : *a,* *b,*
c, *d,* is the table, placed againft the partition X.
The

The branch A B C is joined at A to the prime conductor in the other room ; e and f are two links that come from two chains which communicate with the two fides of a jar or battery, and are concealed in the table.

Fig. 4. The apparatus for conducting electricity from a kite: a is the ftring of the kite, wound upon the reel b ; c is a copper funnel, from which goes the metal rod d, that has a knob ; e is the ftaff that fupports the funnel and reel ; f is the chain by which the electricity is conducted to the ground.

PLATE V. p. 128.

Fig. 1. A B and C D are the poles of two magnets, and the dotted lines fhow the direction of the magnetic effluvia.

Fig. 2 and 3. The magnetic perfpective. In Fig. 3, B is a magnetic needle, placed on an ivory circle C, that refts on the object-glafs D : A is the eye-glafs, by which the pofition of the needle is more clearly diftinguifhed.

Fig. 4. The magnetic wand. C is a magnetic bar, which is inclofed in the hollow wand A B.

PLATE VI. p. 122.

The method of making artificial magnets. Fig. 1, the poker rubbed by the tongs. Fig. 2, 3,

and

and 4, the manner of giving the bars the vertical touch.   Fig. 5, the method of giving them the horizontal touch.   Fig. 6, the manner of difposing the bars in a cafe.

P L A T E VII. p. 140.

Fig. 1. The bouquets, one of which is to be placed in the vafe E, at the bottom of the box A B C D.

Fig. 2. The magnetic dial. A is a circular border that turns quite free on the ftand B; C a dial of pafteboard, that moves in the circular border; l a magnetic needle, which is the index to the dial; P a pin, that fhows where the magnetic bar Fig. 3, is placed, under the dial.

Fig. 4. The dial for the magnetic cards, which is to be placed in the circular border of the laft figure.

P L A T E VIII. p. 148.

Fig. 1. M and N the two boxes for the dexterous painter; T is a pivot, on which the circle of pafteboard F is placed, in the box N; O, P, Q, R, are four boards, on which the fame fubjects are painted as on the pafteboard circle; V is an artificial magnet concealed in each of the boards.

P L A T E

PLATE IX. p. 154.

Fig. 1. The apparatus for the cylindric oracle. ABCD is the cylinder, in which is concealed the magnet H, at E F ; C is a circle to be placed on the cylinder, and has a touched needle for an index.

Fig. 2. The box in which one of the four square pieces Fig. 3, that have each a magnet in a different direction, is to be placed.

Fig. 4. The dial to be placed over the box, Fig. 2.

PLATE X. p. 155.

Fig. 1. An ewer placed on a ftand B, in which is a drawer D.

Fig. 2. The infide of the ewer, in the middle of which is an inverted tin cone: at H is a mirror.

Fig. 3. A pafteboard circle that is placed at Q R in the laft figure. This circle contains a touched needle, and is divided into four parts, in three of which are heads with different dreffes.

Fig. 4. Four fquare pieces of wood, each of which contains a magnet in a different pofition, and in three of them are the fame figures as on the pafteboard.

Fig. 5. The magician's circles. The circle A has a hand that communicates with a movement in the box. The index of the circle B is a

touched

touched needle : C the cross piece by which the two circles are connected.

Fig. 6. The movement contained in the boxes under the two circles, and the cross piece between them.

PLATE XI. p. 168.

Fig. 1. The box and dice. C A a hollow pedestal. on which is the circle B, marked with the numbers on two dice, and at its center is a pivot, on which turns a touched needle; M a similar circle on the bottom of the box; D E is a vase, in which there are different divisions H, G, F. In the part I K is placed the piece S T.

Fig. 2, is a box, in which are placed the two cases Fig. 3 and 4, that have each a magnet at O, and in each of which are placed two flowers; G E O is the section of these two cases.

PLATE XII. p. 176.

Fig. 1. A B C D a box that contains six different pieces of metal, which have each a magnet in a different position.

Fig. 2. The circles that are placed at the end of a perspective, and have the initials of the different metals.

Fig. 3. The box for the magnetic oracle. A, B, C, the three divisions of the box : in A and C are eight small rundlets marked with different numbers.

Fig. 4. The magnets to be fixed in eight small tablets,

tablets, that are to be put in the part B of the laft figure.

Fig. 5. A circle, with a touched needle for an index, which is to be placed on the part B of Fig. 3, over one of the tablets, in which a magnet is concealed.

Fig. 6. A B C D is the box for the magical cards, in the top of which is an opening of the fize of a card. At the center of this box is a pivot, on which is placed a circle that has two cards painted on it, and a touched needle at its center. Between the two figures of the box is the magnetic wand.

P L A T E XIII. p. 180.

Fig. 1. The magnetic planetarium. The central circle has an index A, that communicates with another circle underneath; and round it are wrote feven queftions. Round the feven leffer circles are wrote words that form anfwers to thofe queftions; and within thefe circles are drawn the characters of the five planets, with the earth and moon. On the center of each of thefe circles turns a magnetic needle, and the dotted lines in each of them fhow the pofition of the magnets in feven other circles on the bottom of the box.

Fig. 2, fhows the infide of the box, and the two indexes at top; by the loweft is turned the circle, fixed on a pivot at the bottom of the box; and the other is placed againft one of the months infcribed round the circle. O and P are two of the needles to be placed on the fmall circles.

P L A T E

PLATE XIV. p. 192.

Fig 1 and 2. The magnetical table. ABCD, Fig. 1, the bottom of the table : at A, on the top of the table, is a circle, that surrounds a bason, placed over P, where is the machinery, Fig. 3, which consists of a wheel QR, a barrel X, a small toothed wheel T, and the magnetic bar X Y. MO is a magnetic bar moveable on a pulley, round which goes a string, that is fastened at one end to the spring N, and goes over another pulley at A. OP, at the part of the table next AB, is a magnetic bar, moveable on a pivot at P. The motion of this bar is regulated by the spring R. Round the pulley T goes a string, that passes over another pulley at S. AB, near the part AR, is the magnetic roller, which is drawn backward and forward by a string that passes over the pullies B and A, and is described in Pl. XVII. Fig. 5.

Fig. 2. AB, the top of the table, on which is placed the bason : R, F, G, H, the legs, which are hollow, L, L, the cross pieces, MN the step : these are likewise all hollow, and communicate with the other side of the partition W.

Fig. 3 and 4, are two other circles to be placed round the bason on the table.

PLATE XV. p. 189.

The scale to be placed against the back of the partition W. C is the pulley over which the string

ſtring goes ; D the weight; and E F the index. The diviſions of this ſcale correſpond to thoſe on the three circles in the laſt plate, Fig. 1, 4, and 5.

PLATE XVI. p. 204.

The apparatus for the ſagacious ſwan. Fig. 1. YX a hollow pedeſtal, on which is placed the baſon A, and round it are ſix vaſes ; B is a hollow egg, placed on a ſtand C, that is alſo hollow ; MAO is the magnet and wheel placed in the pedeſtal. The figures *a* ſhow the poſition of the vaſes.

Fig. 2. The machinery for moving the magnet, which is regulated by one of the etwees Y, and the cylinder F, Fig. 3, placed in the egg B and the ſtand C.

PLATE XVII. p. 220.

Fig. 1. The communicative bell. A B a copper box, E the inſide of the box, F the bell, D a magnet, that is placed on a pivot, and ſtrikes the bell.

Fig. 2. The magnetic balance, the ſcales of which are to be placed over the magnetic table at the part where is the magnet M O.

Fig. 3. The movement of the ſympathetic dials. ABCD the wheels and pinions, under which is the barrel A, F the fly, H the plate to which the

move-

movement is fixed, LNM a catch of steel that is touched.

Fig. 4. QR is a case in which each of the dials is to be placed.

Fig. 5. The magnetic roller, in the twelve circles of which are placed magnets in different positions, marked with the letters of the alphabet.

PLATE XVIII. p. 232.

Fig. 1. The magician's box. A B is the base of the box, in the top of which is a hole E, about the size of a card : in this base is placed the circle OP, Fig. 3, that has five cards painted on it ; contains a magnet QR, and is moveable on a pivot.

Fig. 2, is the body of the box, which consists of four inclined planes of glass ; and in a hole at the top V, is fixed a convex lens. This box is placed on the magnetic table, by which either of the cards on the circle are brought under the hole.

Fig. 4. The mystical dial : this dial is divided into ten equal parts, and at its center is a touched needle, which is regulated by the magnetic table.

Fig. 5. The box for the intelligent fly. At the center of the box is a pivot, on which is placed a touched needle L, that has at one end of it an enamelled fly ; over this needle is placed the pasteboard circle A B C D, on which ten letters are wrote.

PLATE

PLATE XIX. p. 238.

Fig. 1. The box with the eight tablets, on which are wrote the multifarious verse, and in each of which is concealed a magnet, in a different direction.

Fig. 2. A board of the same size of the foregoing box, on which are drawn eight circles that have each the same words wrote round them as are on the tablets; and on the center of each of these circles is fixed a magnetic needle; this board is to be placed over the box.

Fig. 3. Four plates of glass, placed in an inclined position over the board, and in its top are two lenses O, O.

PLATE XX. p. 246.

Fig. 1. The communicative mirror. A B is a hollow pedestal, in which is a hole at L, and over that is placed a stand, composed of four plates of glass C D, and on that is fixed a tube E, including another tube F. There is a hole through the tubes, next the top of the stand, and against it is placed an inclined mirror M, by which the eye at G sees the pasteboard circle Fig. 2, fixed on a pivot at the bottom of the box.

Fig. 3. A box of the same size as the pedestal just described. In this box is placed one of the three tablets X, Y, Z, that have each a magnet in a different position, and over each of them is pasted

4   ed

ed a card of the fame fort with thofe on the circle. When this box is placed in the pedeftal, the needle in the circle conforms to the pofition of the magnet in the tablet.

Fig. 4. The box of dice by reflection. ABCD the box, whofe top and fides are of glafs. I L two hollow cubes.   At the end of the box are fliders that draw up as in Fig. 5, and at M is a fmall moveable piece that covers a hole.   O P, and R Q, are two inclined mirrors placed in the box.   The bottom of each of the cubes is divided into four equal parts, as in Fig. 8, and under each of them is placed a brafs ftand, Fig. 6, difpofed as in Fig. 7, and on the ftand is a pivot that holds two needles, one of brafs, the other of fteel that is touched.

R A T I O N A L

RATIONAL RECREATIONS.

ELECTRICITY.

DEFINITIONS.

1. ELECTRICITY is that property in bodies which enables them, when excited by friction or heat, to attract other light bodies, and produce an effluvium that is sometimes luminous, attended with a snapping noise, and a faint phosphoreal smell.

2. Electricity is called the second of the three species of attraction, gravity being the first, and magnetism the third.

3. Those bodies that produce electricity by friction or heat, are called electrics, and are said to be electric *per se*.

4. Those bodies that receive and com-

muni-

municate electricity are called conductors, and those that repel it are called non-conductors.

5. All bodies that are made to contain more than their natural quantity of electricity are said to be electrified positively, and those from whom part of their natural quantity is taken away, are said to be electrified negatively.   These two electricities being first produced, one of them from glass, and the other from amber or rosin, the former was called vitreous, and the latter resinous electricity.

6. When a quantity of electricity is communicated to any body, it is said to be charged.

7. The effect of the explosion of a charged body, that is, the discharge of its electricity on any other body, it is called the electric shock.

8. When any body is prevented from communicating with the earth, by the interposition of an electric body, it is said to be insulated.

9. The

9. The refiduum of a charged body, as a jar or battery, is that part of the charge which remains in the body after the firft difcharge, and by which it will give a fecond fhock, though lefs than the firft.

APHORISMS.

1. All fubftances are diftinguifhed into electrica *per fe*, and non-electrics : the latter of which are conductors, and the former non-conductors.

2. All kinds of metals, femi-metals, water, charcoal, and other bodies of a fimilar nature, are conductors ; and all other bodies, whether mineral, vegetable, or animal, are non-conductors : many of the latter, however, may be made to conduct electricity by being heated to a certain degree.

3. Pofitive electricity is produced by the friction of uninfulated glafs tubes or globes ; and negative electricity is produced, either from the rubber of thofe

bodies,

bodies, or from the friction of infulated glafs bodies; or laftly, from the rubbing of globes or fticks of wax, fulphur, and other bodies of a fimilar nature.

4. It follows from the laft aphorifm that the electricity of the excited body and the rubber, are always oppofite, that is, if that of the excited body be pofitive, that of the rubber will be negative; and the contrary. Thofe two bodies, moreover, will act on each other with greater force than any other body.

5. In charging any body, as a coated phial, if one fide communicate with the excited body, and the other with the rubber, the electricity of the two fides of the charged body will be oppofite.

6. There is a ftrong attraction between the two electricities on the oppofite fides of a glafs, fo that when they are made to communicate by means of a conductor, they will be both difcharged with a flafh of light and a fnapping noife.

7. The fubftance of glafs is impervious

to

to electricity; but if the glafs be thin, and the electricity on the oppofite fides be very ftrong, that is, if the glafs be overcharged, the oppofite electricities will force a paffage through the glafs.

8. If an excited electric be in contact with an infulated conductor, the former will communicate its power to the latter, which will then attract light bodies, and give a fhock, in the fame manner as the excited electric.

9. The flafh of light from a body to which electricity has been communicated, is more denfe, and the found louder, than from one that is excited; for the conductor parts with all its electricity at once, but the excited body with only fo much as is at, or near, the part that is touched.

10. If infulated bodies have been attracted by, and have touched an excited body, they will, foon after, be repelled by that body, and will repel each other; nor will they return to the excited electric till after they

have

have touched some other body that communicates with the earth.

11. When an insulated conductor is brought within the sphere of action of an excited body, it requires the electricity opposite to that of the body, and the nearer it is brought the greater quantity it acquires, till the one receive a spark from the other, and then the electricity of both is discharged.

12. The electric explosion always takes the shortest course through the best conductors,

13. If the explosion between two bodies be interrupted by a non-conductor of a moderate density, the discharge will force a passage through it, in such manner as to leave the appearance of a sudden expansion of the air about the center of the explosion.

14. If an insulated conductor be pointed, or if an uninsulated conductor that is pointed, be brought very near the earth, there will be no other appearance of electricity

tricity during the time of excitation, than a light, and a current of air, that may be perceived to come from thofe points.

15. The electric attraction acts in vacuo.

16. Electricity and lightning are in all refpects of a fimilar nature. All the effects of lightning may be imitated by electricity, and all the experiments in electricity may be performed by lightning, brought down from the clouds by means of an infulated pointed rod of metal.

ELEC-

ELECTRICAL APPARATUS.

A Defcription of all the machinery that has been ufed in electrical experiments, would fill a large volume. We fhall here confine ourfelves to fuch as are of general ufe, and neceffary, in particular, to the following recreations : fuch are the re-volving globe and rubber, with its prime conductor, ufually called an electric ma-chine ; the electric battery ; the fulmineous conductor ; and the electrometer.

The conftruction of the electric machine is as follows *. Let *a a*, Plate I. be two

---

* A great number of different electrical ma-chines have been contrived. This appears to be the invention of Dr. Prieftley, from whofe Hiftory of Electricity we have extracted the defcription of the following apparatus, and the fubfequent recre-ations, fome few articles excepted ; for that va-luable work contains every material difcovery or improvement that has been hitherto made in this fcience. A machine of a more fimple conftruction will be defcribed further on.

ftrong

ftrong boards of mahogany, the lower about an inch on each side broader than the other: they are to be an equal length, parallel with each other, and about four inches afunder. In the upper board is a groove, that goes almoft its whole length. The pillars are of baked wood: that marked *b* is immoveable, being fixed to the upper and lower boards; the other flides in the groove juft mentioned, that it may receive globes or cylinders of different dimenfions *, but is only neceffary when they have axes. In each of the pillars there are holes at equal diftances, by means of which the globes may be placed at a height adapted to their bulk. These pil-

---

* It is not yet determined what fort of glafs is moft proper for thefe globes and cylinders. The beft flint is commonly ufed, but Dr. Prieftley feems to think, that common bottle metal is the moft eligible. Some operators line their globes or cylinders with wax, or fome other electric fubftance; which in large globes may be of good ufe; but when they are fmall, no material advantage can be expected from any lining.

lars

lars are to be high enough to admit
two or more globes at the same time. If
two globes be fixed on one axis, four of a
moderate size may be used, and the wheel
may have several grooves for that purpose.
When a globe with one neck is used, as
in the plate, a brafs arm *c*, with an open
focket, is neceffary to fupport the axis
beyond the pulley : this part is alfo contrived to put higher or lower, together
with the brafs focket in which the axis
turns. The axis *d*, is made to come
quite through the pillar, that it may be
turned by a handle, without the wheel, at
the option of the operator. As the frame
ferews to the table, it may be placed at different diftances from the wheel, in proportion to the length of the ftring, in different
ftates of the air. The wheel is fixed
in a feparate frame *e*, by which means
it may be placed in any fituation, with refpect to the pulley, and be turned to one
fide, fo as to prevent the parts of the
ftring from cutting each other. The back

part

part of this frame is supported by a separate foot *.

The rubber *f*, confists of a hollow piece of copper, ftuffed with horfe hair, and covered with a bafil fkin. It is fupported by a focket, that receives the cylindrical axis of a round, flat piece of baked wood *g*, the oppofite part of which is inferted into the focket of a bent fteel fpring *h* †. Thefe parts are eafily feparated; fo that the rubber, and the piece of wood by which it is infulated, may be

* Some electric machines are turned by a brafs toothed wheel and pinion, inclofed in a box, which has a more elegant appearance; but thefe wheels are fubject to accidents, which are not fo eafily repaired as thofe that happen to a ftring.

† If the rubber be very narrow, fome parts of the globe will pafs without a fufficient friction: to remedy this inconvenience the hand, when dry, may be held to the globe, juft before the rubber, to fupply the deficiency. There fhould be no fharp edges or angles about the rubber, for they would make its infulation, which is a matter of great confequence, ineffectual.

changed

changed at pleasure. The position of the spring may be altered two ways: it may either be slipped along the groove, or moved in the contrary direction, so as to give it every desireable position with re-gard to the globe or cylinder: and it is, besides, furnished with a screw *i*, which makes it press harder or lighter, as the experiment may require.

The prime conductor *k* *, is a hollow vessel of polished copper, in the form of a

---

* For common purposes a small conductor is most convenient; but when a strong spark is wanted, it is proper to have a large conductor ready, which may be placed in contact with the smaller. But whatever be the size of the con-ductor, that part which is most remote from the globe should be round, and much larger than the rest: for the effort of the electric matter to fly off, is always the greatest at the greatest distance from the globe; and from that part the longest and strongest sparks may be drawn.

The largest and most pungent sparks are drawn from any conductor along an electric substance. Thus if the conductor be supported by pillars of

glass

pear, supported by a pillar, on a firm basis of baked wood*; and it receives its

glafs or baked wood, the longeft fparks will be taken clofe to the pillar.

If part of the conductor be concave, a remarkable large, ftrong, and undivided fpark may be drawn from the concavity. Where the furface is convex, the fpark is more apt to be weak and divided.

* Baked wood is found by experience to form a perfect nfulation, but it requires to be baked again at different times, efpecially if it be kept in a damp fituation. A hollow pillar of glafs, lined with fealing wax, will anfwer exceeding well, and does not require fo much attention. The beft method of lining a glafs is to diffolve fo much fealing-wax, in fpirit of wine, as will make it of a due confiftence. It may then be laid on the glafs, by a brufh, with very little trouble.

Dr. Prieftley advifes electricians to make all their ftands and ftools for infulation, of baked wood; as it may be eafily turned into any form; as it infulates better than glafs, and is not fo brittle. But care muft be taken that the wood be thoroughly baked, even till it be quite brown: it will not then be very apt to collect moifture from the air: if it fhould, a little warming and rubbing will be fufficient to expel that moifture. At moft, it can only be necessary to boil it in linfeed oil, or give it a flight coating of varnifh after it comes out of the oven.

electricity by means of a long arched wire, or rod of very soft brass *l*, easily bent into any shape, and raised higher or lower as the globe may require : it is terminated by an open ring, in which are hung some sharp-pointed wires or needles *m*, that play lightly on the globe when it is in motion.

The body of the conductor is furnished with holes and sockets, for the insertion of metallic rods, to convey the fire wherever it is wanted ; and for many other purposes, incident to a course of electrical experiments. The conductor is by this mean steady, and yet may be easily put into any situation. It collects the fire perfectly well, and (what is of the greatest consequence, though but little regarded) retains it equally every where.

oven. When this preparation is used, it must be well heated once more, immediately after the boiling.

When

When positive electricity is wanted, a wire or chain, as is represented in the plate at n, connects the rubber with the table, or floor. When negative electricity is wanted, that wire is connected with another conductor, such as that represented at n, Pl. II. while the conductor in Pl. I. is connected, by another wire or chain, with the table. If the rubber be made tolerably free from points, the negative power will be as strong as the positive.

The principal advantages of this machine are, that glafs veffels, or any other electric body, of any fize or form, may be ufed, either with one or two necks. All the effential parts of the machine, as the globe, the frame, the wheel, the rubber, and the conductor, are quite feparate, and the pofition of them to each other may be varied in every manner poffible. The rubber has a complete infulation, by which mean the operator may command either the negative or pofitive power, and may change

change them in an inftant. This conductor is fteady, and eafily enlarged, by
placing rods in the holes with which it
is furnifhed, or by the conjunction of other
conductors, in order to give larger fparks,
&c. It may be turned either with or
without the wheel, fo that the operator
may fit or ftand to his work, at his option;
and he may, with the utmoft eafe, manage
both the machine and the other parts of
the apparatus *.

When the air is dry, particularly when
there is a froft, and the wind is north or

* We are informed that Dr. Prieftley, fince the
publication of his Hiftory, has contrived a windmill,
to be placed on the top of his houfe, by which
his electrical machine is occafionally turned. One
or more globes excited by the force of a ftrong
wind, muft doubtlefs produce a very great quantity of electricity; and from that gentleman's ex-
tenfive knowledge of this fcience, and his un-
wearied application to the improvement of experimental philofophy, the learned world has reafon to
hope for fome further important difcoveries in electricity.

eaft,

PLATE. I

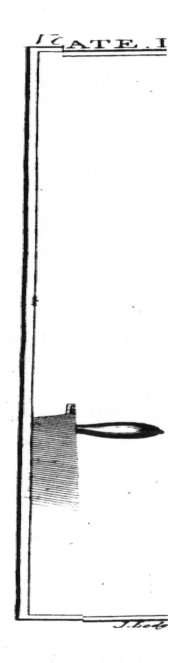

J. Lodg.

eaft, there is fcarce any electric machine but will work very well. If the air be damp, make a large fire in the room where the machine ftands, and let the globe, and every thing about it, be made very dry : it will then work almoft as well as in the beft ftate of the air.

To increafe the quantity of electric fire from a globe, let the rubber be a little moiftened, from time to time ; or rather, moiften the under fide of a loofe piece of leather, that may occafionally be put upon the rubber. But the moft powerful exciter is a little amalgam, made by rubbing mercury and thin pieces of lead or tinfoil together, in the palm of the hand. If a rubber be at any time placed perpendicular to the horizon, it will be neceffary to ufe a little tallow to make it ftick. With this excellent refource, almoft all forts of weather become equally fit for electrical experiments.

A little

A little time after fresh amalgam has been put upon the rubber, and often at other times, if there be any foulness upon the cushion, and sometimes when there is none, there will be found upon the globe, small black spots, of a hard rough substance, which grow continually larger, till a considerable quantity of that matter be accumulated upon the surface. This must be carefully picked off, or it will obstruct the excitation, and in a great measure defeat the intended operation.

When the amalgam has been used for some time, there will be formed upon the rubber, a thick incrustation of the same kind of black substance that is apt to adhere to the globe. This incrustation is a very great improvement of the rubber; for when once a considerable body of it is formed, and it is a little moistened or scraped, as much fire will be produced if fresh amalgam were used; so that it seems to supersede the further use of the amalgam.

As

As the electric matter is collected only at the rubber, it is neceſſary that it have a communication with the common maſs of the earth, by means of good conductors. If, therefore, the table on which the machine ſtands, or the floor of the room in which it is uſed, be very dry, little or no fire will be got, be the machine ever ſo good. In this caſe it will be neceſſary to connect the rubber, by means of chains or wires, with the floor, the ground, or even the next water, if the neighbouring ground be dry.

If the conductor be made perfectly well, and the air be dry, there will never be any loſs of fire from any part of it ; for when the whole ſurface has received as high a charge as the machine can give, it will, in all places alike, perfectly reſiſt all efforts to throw any more upon it, and the circulation of the fluid by the rubber will be ſtopped, being balanced, as it were, by equal forces. Or if it loſe, in all places

alike,

alike, the diffipation muft be invifible. This maxim almoft admits of ocular de- monftration; for when the rubber is per- fectly infulated, and the conductor has an opportunity of difcharging itfelf, the rub- ber will take fparks from a wire placed near it, very faft; but when the conductor has but little opportunity of difcharging itfelf, it will take fewer of thofe fparks.

The larger the conductor is, the ftronger fparks it will give: for the greater the electric furface, the greater quantity of the electric atmofphere it contains, and the more fenfible its effect will be, when it is all difcharged at once. The conductor, however, may be made fo large, that the neceffary diffipation of the electric matter from its furface into the air, will be equal to the fupply from the machine, which will conftitute the maximum of the power of that machine, and which will be dif- ferent in different ftates of the air.

To

To form a juft eftimate of the electric power of different machines, take two wires, with knobs of any fize, and fix one of them at the conductor of one of the machines, and the other wire about an inch or an inch and a half from it; and as the wheel turns, count the number of fparks that pafs between them in any given time. Fix the fame wires to the conductor of another machine (but if the fame conductor were ufed the trial would be more exact) and the difference between the number of fparks in the given time will determine the difference of ftrength in the two machines*.

* For common purpofes there are electric machines conftructed without either globe, cylinder, or wheel, as thus : let two upright pieces of wood, of about two feet long, be joined at bottom by a crofs piece, and let there be a gripe to faften them to a table, or any horizontal board. Againft the infide of each of the perpendicular pieces fix a leather cufhion, and let there be a hole made thro' each piece and cufhion, oppofite to each other. Then take a plate of glafs, about a foot fquare, and polifhed on both fides, through the middle of

which

The electric machine being thus completely adjufted, the operator will next want metal rods to conduct, and coated glafs jars or phials to retain and communicate the electric fire. Metallic rods, fuch as *s*, Plate II. ufed in taking fparks from the conductor, for various purpofes, fhould have knobs, of different dimenfions,

which let a workman make a hole, of the fame fize with thofe in the pofts and cufhions : if thefe holes be about nine inches from the top, you may work the machine either fitting or ftanding. Thro' all the holes let an axis be paffed, that has a handle at one end. The cufhions are to prefs hard againft the glafs.

Next, provide a conductor, which may confift of a fmall iron rod, faftened by fealing-wax to an upright piece of wood, fupported by a glafs veffel of any fort; from the rod muft go a wire, at the end of which are to be two large needles, that communicate with the two fides of the glafs ; and from each of the rubbers there muft go a chain to the floor or table. When pofitive electricity is wanted, the needles are to communicate with the glafs ; and when negative electricity, with the cufhions. With this machine and a little care and practice, you will be enabled to perform all the common operations in electricity.

in

in proportion to the curvature of the conductor. If the knob be too fmall, it will
not difcharge the conductor at once, but
by degrees, and with a lefs fenfible effect ;
whereas the fpark between broad furfaces
is thick and ftrong.

The moft formidable part of the electric apparatus is the coated glafs, ufed in
the Leyden experiment * and the battery.
The form of the glafs is immaterial with
refpect to the fhock ; but for different experiments both plates and jars, of various
fhapes and fizes, muft be ufed. The moft
commodious form, for common ufe, is
that of a jar, as wide as a perfon can conveniently grafp, and as tall as will ftand
without danger of falling : perhaps about
three inches and a half diameter, and
about eight inches high. The mouth

* By the Leyden experiment is here meant the
fhock that is given by two wires, communicating
with the two fides of a charged coated glafs or
phial.

C 4

fhould

should be pretty open, that it may be the more conveniently coated on the inside, as well as on the outside, with tinfoil : but it will be generally most convenient to have the mouth narrower than the belly, for then it may more easily be kept clean and dry, and the cork, when one is wanted, will be easier to manage. A jar thus prepared, of a moderate size, is called the Leyden phial. But no electrician should be without jars of various forms and sizes. The figures of several of them are expressed in Plate II. at *c, d, e, f, g, h, i, j,* and *k.* The form of a plated coat of glass is represented at *b.*

The practice of coating jars is far preferable to that of putting water, or brass shavings, into them, which not only makes them heavy, but incapable of being inverted, which is requisite in many experiments. Brass dust, or leaden shot, are, however, very convenient for small phials, and serve very well where it is necessary to remove the

PLATE. II.

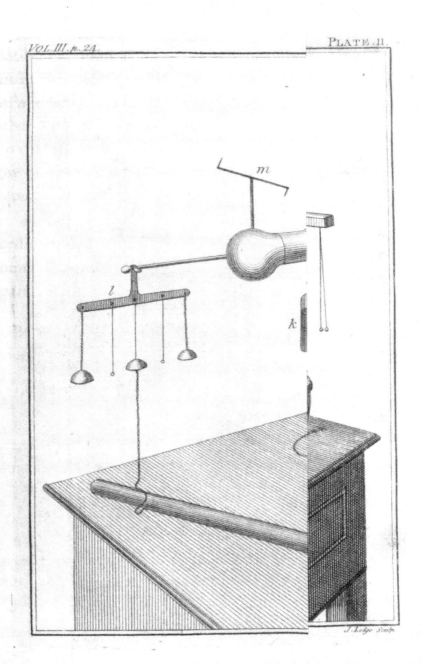

J. Lodge Sculp.

coating as foon as the jar as is charged, but in this cafe quickfilver will generally anfwer beft. The tinfoil may be put on either with pafte, gum-water, or bees wax. To coat the infide of veffels that have narrow mouths, moiften the infide with gumwater, and then pour fome brafs duft upon it: enough will ftick on to make an exceeding good coating, and will not eafily come off, unlefs fomething very hard rub againft it.

Being thus provided with a machine to produce, and jars to receive the electric matter, it will be proper, in the next place, to conftruct an electrometer, that you may know when your jars are fufficiently charged *. There have been

* The moft effectual method of charging a jar, is to connect the outfide, by means of wires, with the rubber, while the wire, proceeding from the infide, is in contact with the conductor. In this manner the infide of the jar will be fupplied with the very fame fire that left the outfide. In this cafe alfo the jar will receive as high a charge as it is capable

many different inventions for this purpofe. That of Mr. Cauton is one of the
moſt ſimple, and is uſeful on many occa-
ſions. It conſiſts of two pieces of cork,
or pith of elder, nicely turned in a lathe,
to about the ſize of a ſmall pea, and ſuſpended on fine linen threads, repreſented
at *c*, Plate II. on a glaſs, ſtanding on a
ſtool. It is convenient to place them in a
ſmall box for the pocket; the box ſhould
be the full length of the ſtrings, that they
may lie in it without being bent *. Theſe

pable of receiving, though the rubber be inſulated,
and have no communication but with the outſide
coating; ſo that in the caſe of charging, there can
be no occaſion for the directions given above,
when the table, the floor, or the ground are very
dry. When a thin jar is diſcharged, it is adviſe-
able not to do it by placing the diſcharging rod oppoſite the thinneſt part, as it will endanger the
burſting of the jar in that part.

* If a ſmooth cork ball be hung on a long
ſtring of ſilk, and electrified poſitively, it will always be repelled by poſitive, and attracted by negative electricity: but the ſtrongeſt repulſion will be
changed into attraction at a certain diſtance.

balls

balls not only fhow when a jar has a fufficient charge, but alfo difcover a very
fmall degree of electricity, and mark its
changes from pofitive to negative, and the
contrary *.

* If two pith-balls, hung by linen threads, and
diverging with pofitive electricity, be infulated;
though in connection with conductors of confiderable length, the approach of a body electrified pofitively, will firft make them feparate, and then (if
the electricity of the balls be fmall, and that of the
approaching body great) it will, at a certain diftance, make them approach, and at length come
into contact with it.   Sometimes the divergence,
previous to the convergence, is very fmall, and,
without great attention, is apt to be over-
looked.

If the balls have a free communication with the
earth, for inftance, if they be held in the hand of
a perfon ftanding on the ground, and (as in the
former cafe) they be made to diverge with pofitive
electricity, in confequence of being held within
the influence of a body electrified negatively, the
approach of pofitive electricity will make them
converge ; and negative electricity, diverge : the
electric matter of the approaching body, in the
former cafe, repelling that of the balls, and thereby, as it were, unelectrifying them ; whereas, in
                                                    the

But the moſt ſenſible of all electrome-
ters conſiſts of two or three threads of
ſilk, as they come from the worm, to which
is faſtened a piece of down, that is juſt ſufficient to keep them perpendicular to the
horizon. If inſulation be neceſſary, faſten
them to a piece of baked wood. When
the ends of theſe threads have received a
ſmall degree of electricity, they will retain
it a conſiderable time, and the ſlighteſt electric force will put them in motion *. But
before any experiment be made, it will
be proper to obſerve carefully, how long
they will retain the degree of electricity
that is intended to be given them, in any

the latter caſe, the negative electricity of an approaching body, draws it more powerfully into the
threads, and makes them diverge more. This method of judging is, therefore, excellently adapted to
aſcertain the kind of electricity in the atmoſphere,
or of a charged jar or battery ; the balls being
held in the hand of a perſon ſtanding on the earth
or floor.

* Theſe threads will diſcover a ſmaller degree of
electricity than can be eaſily perceived by the
balls.

ſituafituation, and a proportionable allowance is to be made in the courfe of the experiments.

The only inftrument, however, that can with propriety be called an electrometer, that is, fuch as meafures the precife degree to which any body is electrified, was invented by Mr. Henly, and is defcribed in the Philofophical Tranfactions, in a letter from Dr. Prieftley to Dr. Franklin, and is ae follows: A (Plate IV. Fig. 1.) is a very light rod, that turns on the center of a femicircle B, fo as always to keep pretty near its graduated limb: at the extremity of the rod is a cork ball C.   D is the pillar that fupports the rod, and may be either fixed to the prime conductor, or let into the brafs knob of a jar or battery, or be fet on a ftand to fupport itfelf.   The whole inftrument may be made of wood or ivory, but is found moft perfect when the pillar and rod, or index, are of box, made very fmooth with emery paper: the ball of cork,

and

2

and the femicircle ivory, as the divifions on that are more legible than on wood.

The moment this inftrument begins to be electrified, the rod is repelled by the pillar, and confequently begins to move over the edge of the femicircle, and fhows, to the greateft precifion, the degree to which the prime conductor is electrified; or how high any jar or battery is charged. As the materials of which this inftrument are made are very imperfect conductors, it will very rarely diffipate any of the electricity of the prime conductor, &c. with which it is connected : but if it be found, by a trial in the dark, that any part of it collects the electric matter, it muft be placed before, the fire to dry off the damp, particularly from the index : it fhould not, however, be much heated, for then it will not receive the electricity ready enough, and the motion of the index will not anfwer with fufficient accuracy, to the degree of electricity in the body with which it is

in

in contact : but this inconvenience may be eafily remedied by moiftening the pillar and the index ; for the femicircle can never be too dry.

It is evident, from the conftruction of this inftrument, that the force of different explofions may be afcertained by it, before the difcharge, with the greateft accuracy. If a jar be charged with pofitive electricity, and you want to know the precife time, while you are attempting to charge it negatively, that it becomes difcharged, watch the moment the index comes to the perpendicular ftation, which may be obferved without the leaft danger of a miftake, and you will then find there is not the leaft fpark left in the jar. If you continue the operation, the index will begin to advance again ; and thereby fhow the exact quantity of the oppofite electricity the jar has acquired.

The

The electrical battery is compofed of a number of coated jars, enclofed in a cafe, as in Fig. 2. Plate III. Very large jars are not the moft eligible ; thofe that are fmaller contain a greater coated furface in propor-tion to their bulk ; and it is by that the force of a battery is produced. The largeft jars that can be conveniently made are about 17 inches high, and they fhould not be more than 3 inches in diameter, and every where of an equal width.

The battery ufed and recommended by Dr. Prieftley, confifts of 64 glafs jars*, each 10 inches high, and two inches and a half diameter, and coated to within one inch and a half of the top (fee Plate III). The coated part of each is, therefore, half a fquare foot ; fo that the whole battery con-tains 32 fquare feet. The wire of each

* A lefs number, however, will be quite fuf-ficient for common purpofes : on the contrary, where a very great force is wanted, two or more batteries may be connected, and feparate jars added to them.

jar

jar has a piece of very fmall wire twifted about the lower end of it, to touch the infide coating in feveral places, and it is put through a pretty large piece of cork, within the jar, to prevent any part of it touching the fide, which would tend to promote a fpontaneous difcharge *. Each wire is turned round, fo as to make a hole at the upper end, and through thefe holes is put a pretty thick brafs rod with knobs; one rod ferving for one row of the jars.

The communication between thefe rods is made by laying over all of them a chain, which is not drawn in the plate, left the figure fhould appear confufed. When you would ufe only a part of the battery, you lay the chain over as many rods as you want rows of jars. The bottom of

---

* Inftead of this wire with a cork, the jars of fome batteries have wires bent double, whofe lower parts are fprings, fo that they touch the fides of the jar next the bottom, without coming near the top.

the box in which thefe jars ftand, is covered with tin-foil and brafs duft; and a
bent wire, touching the tin-foil, is put
through the box, and appears on the outfide, as in the figure. To this wire is
faftened whatever is intended to communicate with the outfide of the battery, as
the piece of fmall wire in the figure; and
the difcharge is made by bringing the brafs
knob to any of the knobs of the battery.
The glafs of which this battery is made,
is what the workmen call flint green, which
Dr. Prieftley thinks much better for this
purpofe than the beft flint, as jars made
of it are not fo apt to difcharge themfelves; and it is moreover much cheaper.

In order to judge of the ftrength of a
charge, (which in large batteries is a matter of confiderable confequence) apply the
electrometer to the wires, from time to
time. A comparifon of the degree of the
divergence of the balls, compared with the
actual explofion, will foon enable the
oper-

operator to tell how high his battery is charged, and consequently what will be the force of the explosion.

You are not to conclude, because you can touch the wires of a large battery without any effect, that therefore, while your hand is upon them, you can safely touch the outside coating with the other hand ; for sometimes when the wires have shown no signs of a charge, and even two days after the battery has been discharged, very violent shocks have been received. Therefore, soon after the first explosion, it is proper to discharge the residuum for fear of a disagreeable accident. When the box is very dry, there will sometimes remain even the residuum of a residuum, for several days.

The best construction of a fulmineous conductor, that is, a machine to draw down electricity or lightning from the clouds, is as follows. On the top of any building, (which

D 2   will

will be more convenient if it stand on an eminence) erect a pole *a* (Plate IV. Fig. 2.) as tall as a man can well manage, having on its top a solid piece of glass, or baked wood, a foot long; over which fix a tin or copper veffel *b*, in form of a funnel, to preferve it conftantly from the rain; above this let there rife a long flender rod *c*, terminating in a pointed wire, and having a fmall wire twifted round its whole length, to conduct the electricity the better to the funnel. From the funnel let a wire *d*, defcend along the building, at about a foot diftance from it, and be conducted through an open fafh, into the room that is moft convenient for performing the experiments. In this room let a proper conductor be infulated, and connected with the wire that comes in at the window. This wire and conductor being completely infulated, will be electrified whenever there is a confiderable quantity of electricity in the air; and notice will be given when it is properly charged,

.either

either by the pith balls hung to it, or by
such a set of bells as will be hereafter
described.

To make experiments with this apparatus in perfect safety, the electrified wire
should be brought within a few inches of
a conducting rod, which serves to guard
the house, that the redundant electricity
may pass off that way, without striking
any person who may chance to stand near
it. The conductor to guard the house
should consist of one rod, between one-
fourth and one-half of an inch thick, if it
be of iron, but smaller, if it be of brass or
copper, and terminating upward in a sharp
point, about four or five feet above the
highest part of the building ; and below, it
should, if possible, be continued to some
well or running water; if not, it should
be sunk several feet into the ground,
at the distance of some yards from the
building. It is of no consequence whether this conducting rod be fastened to the

inside

inside or outside of the house, or how many bendings there are in it.

Beside these principal parts of an electrical apparatus, the operator will frequently find it very convenient, when only small quantities of electricity are required, to be provided with tubes and cylinders of glass, and sticks of wax or sulphur.

Glass tubes should be made as long as a person can well draw through his hand at one stroke, that is, about three feet, or something more, and as wide as can be conveniently grasped. It is not necessary that the glass be thick; perhaps the thinner the better, if it will bear sufficient friction, which however need be but very gentle, when the tube is in good order. It is most convenient to have the tube closed at one end; for the electric matter is not only thereby best retained on its surface, but the air may be more easily drawn out, or condensed in it, by means of of a brafs cap fitted to the open end. A tube thus furnifhed is reprefented at *a*, Plate II. and is requifite for various experiments.

The beft rubber for a fmooth glafs tube is the rough fide of black oiled filk, efpecially when a little amalgam of mercury and any metal, is put upon it. A little bees wax drawn over the furface of a tube will alfo greatly increafe its power. In rubbing a tube, the hand fhould be kept two or three inches below the upper part of the rubber, otherwife the electricity will difcharge itfelf upon the hand, and nothing will remain upon the tube for the experiment. When the tube is in very good order, and ftrongly excited, it will throw off many pencils of rays at every ftroke, without the approach of any conductor, except what may float in the common atmofphere.

D 4

An

An electrician should also be furnished with rough glass tubes, that is, such as have their polish taken off; though a cylinder of baked wood will do nearly as well. The best rubber for a rough glass tube, or a cylinder of baked wood, as well as for a stick of wax or sulphur, is soft new flannel; or rather skins, such as hare or cat-skin, tanned with the hair on, being smoother, and having a more exquisite polish.

Such is the common construction of an electrical apparatus; but to make this part of our work correspond with the rest, by adding surprise to learning and ingenuity, it will be necessary to conceal the apparatus, by placing it in an adjoining room. For which purpose, let the table *a*, *b*, *c*, *d*, (Plate IV. Fig. 3.) be placed against the partition X, that separates the two rooms. Let the branch ABC be joined at A to the prime conductor in the other room: round the part A must be a piece of wood, baked

and

and prepared as is defcribed in the account of the apparatus; this piece muft be made to take out, that it may be heated by the fire, in damp weather, before the exhibition begins; and muft be nicely fitted to the wainfcot, that it may not occafion fufpicion of any communication. The knob at C muft be larger than ufual, that it may give the larger fnap. The branch being thus joined to the prime conductor, will anfwer all the purpofes of the conductor itfelf, and larger fnaps will be taken from C, than from any part near the globe.

In each fide of the top of the table, between *a e* and *b f*, muft be concealed a glafs tube that communicates with the other room, and in thefe tubes muft be placed the two chains that come from the two fides of a jar or battery, only one link of which, however, is to be feen at *e* and *f*, which may appear as hooks faftened to the table: to thefe hooks two other chains

chains or wires are to be faftened, when an explofion is wanted.

Certain words or phrafes muft be agreed on between the operator and his affiftant, by which the latter may know when he is to charge the conductor, or connect the chains with the jar or battery. There fhould likewife be a fmall hole in the partition, by which he may guide himfelf with more certainty. Under the table may be a drawer, that may be pulled out occafionally, to fhow that there is nothing concealed.

To the foregoing apparatus it may be proper to add fome account of the tourmalin, a fubftance that has been ufed in electric experiments but a few years paft, but is fuppofed to be the lyncurium of the ancients, to which they attributed fome electric properties. This ftone is common in feveral parts of the Eaft, and particularly

larly in the island of Ceylon, from whose
inhabitants it received its present name.*

The tourmalin is a fossil of a hard and
very compact substance, of a deep red colour,
and pellucid. Its principal properties are
thus described by Mr. Canton, in the Gentleman's Magazine for September 1759.

1. When the tourmalin is not electrical,
or attractive, heating it, without friction,
will make it so; and the electricity of one
side of it (distinguished by A) will be positive, and that of the other side (B) will
be negative.

2. The tourmalin not being electrical,
will become so by cooling; but with this
difference, that the side A will be negative,
and the side B positive.

3. If the tourmalin, in a non-electric

* Since the use of the tourmalin in electricity,
it has been discovered that some other stones or
gems, particularly the Brazil topaz, have similar
properties.

state,

state, be heated, and suffered to cool again, without either of its sides being touched, A will be positive, and B negative, the whole time of the increase and decrease of its heat.

4. Either side of the tourmalin will be positive by friction, and both may be made so at the same time.

Mr. Canton observed further, that it is not heat, but the circumstance of changing its degree of heat, that gives electricity to this stone.

Dr. Priestley has ingeniously remarked, that a pleasing deception might be made by enclosing a tourmalin, in a thin coat of sealing-wax; for the coat will then seem to have acquired the properties of the tourmalin.

We have been more minute in the description of this apparatus than may seem necessary to the performing the following

recre-

recreations : but it is from the definitions and aphorifms, together with a defcription of the apparatus, that a knowledge of the feveral branches of fcience contained in this work, is to be acquired ; the recreations being principally intended to exemplify what is there laid down. Befide, a perfon of ingenuity, in poffeffion of this electric apparatus, may invent a great number of fimilar recreations; which being the produce of his own mind, will, perhaps, be found more entertaining than any here defcribed ; and at the fame time may, fome of them, tend to the further ecclairciffement of this very pleafing branch of experimental philofophy.

ELEC-

ELECTRICAL RECREATIONS.

We shall divide these Recreations into such as are performed in the light, and such as require a dark chamber; beginning with the former.

RECREATION I.

The animated feather.

ELECTRIFY a smooth glass tube with a rubber, and hold a small feather (or piece of leaf gold) at a short distance from it. The feather will immediately fly to the tube, and adhere to it for a short time, and then fly off; and the tube can never be brought close to the feather till it has touched the side of the room, or some other body that communicates with the ground. If, therefore, the operator take care to keep the tube constantly between the feather and the side of the room, he may drive it round to all parts without touching it; and, what is very remarkable, the fame fide of the feather will be conftantly oppofite the tube.

While the feather is flying before the fmooth tube, it will be immediately attracted by an excited rough tube, or a ftick of wax, and fly continually from one tube to the other, till the electricity of both is difcharged *.

This was one of the firft, and is one of the moft common experiments in electricity; it is however very entertaining, and fhows the nature of electric attraction and repulfion altogether as well as a more elaborate performance.

* This feather not badly reprefents one of that defpicable fort of women they call coquettes; who when an excited fuitor appears, readily flies to him, but prefently quits him. If another fuitor appear, fhe in like manner flies to him, and in like manner leaves him; and then, unlefs a third party appear, is continually changing from one to the other; till at laft, they both grow tired of her, and fhe then remains as infignificant and contemptible as a mere feather.

RECREATION II.

The self-raising pyramid.

PROVIDE a large circular bundle of threads, of different colours, and let the threads be also of different lengths, increasing from the circumference to the center, where they are to be longest. Suspend this bundle from the middle of the brass arch between the pillars (Plate IV. Fig. 3). Then inform the company that the threads will rise up, at their command, in form of a pyramid, and continue in that form as long as they direct, and then return to their first position.

Therefore, when they command the threads to rise, you give the signal to the operator behind the partition, who, by turning the wheel, electrifies the arch, when the threads will immediately rise

up,

up, in form of a pyramid, and continue fo, as long as the operator continues turning the wheel, but when that ftops they will immediately return to their former pofition.

RECREATION III.

The magical dance.

FROM the middle of the brafs arch fufpend three fmall bells, in the fame manner they are fufpended from the end of the conductor in Plate I. at *l.* The two outer bells hang by chains, and that in the middle by a filk ftring, while a chain connects it with the floor. Two fmall knobs of brafs, which ferve as clappers, hang, by filk ftrings, one between each two bells. Therefore when the two outer bells, communicating with the conductor, are electrified, they will attract the clappers, and be ftruck by them. The clappers being thus loaded with elec-

VOL. III.   E   tricity,

tricity, will be repelled, and fly to difcharge themfelves upon the middle bell;
after which, they will be again attracted
by the outer bells: and thus, by ftriking
the bells alternately, the ringing may
be continued as long as the operator
thinks proper *.

The mufic for your dance being thus
provided, you are next to fufpend a plate
of metal from the fame part of the arch
to which the bells are connected: at
the diftance of a few inches from the arch,
and exactly under it, place a metal-ftand of
the fame fize, in the fame manner as at
v and n in Plate II. On the ftand
place feveral figures of men, other animals,
or what you pleafe, cut in paper of leaf

* In the dark a continual flafhing of light will
be feen between the clappers and the bells, and
when the electrification is very ftrong, thefe flafhes
of light will be fo large, that they will be tranfmit-
ted by the clapper from one bell to the other, without its ever coming into actual contact with either
of them; and confequently the ringing will ceafe.

gold,

gold, and pretty sharply pointed at both extremities *.

When the plate that hangs from the arch is electrified, the figures will dance with amazing rapidity, and the bells at the same time ringing inceffantly, will afford no fmall entertainment to the fpectators. This Recreation may be ftopped and renewed at pleafure, in the fame manner as the laft.

* If a piece of leaf gold be cut with a pretty large angle at one extremity, and a very acute angle at the other, it will want no ftand, but will hang, by its larger angle, at a fmall diftance from the conductor, and by the continual waving motion of its lower extremities, will have the appearance of fomething animated, biting or nibbling at the conductor. It is therefore called by Dr. Franklin the Golden Fifh.

RECRE-

RECREATION IV.

The artificial spider.

CUT a piece of burnt cork, about the fize of a pea, into the form of the body of a spider; make its legs of linen thread, and put a grain or two of lead into it, to give it more weight. Sufpend it by a fine line of filk between the electrified arch and an excited ftick of wax, and it will, like a clapper between two bells, jump continually from one body to the other, moving its legs at the fame time, as if animated; to the no fmall furprize of thofe who are unacquainted with the electric influence *.

* This is an American invention, and was firft defcribed by Dr. Franklin.

RECRE-

RECREATION V.

The marvellous fountain.

SUSPEND a veffel of water from the middle of the brafs arch, and place in the veffel a capillary fyphon. The water will at firft iffue by drops only, from the lower leg of the fyphon; but when the wheel is put in motion, there will be one continued ftream of water, and if the electrification be ftrong, a number of ftreams will iffue, in form of a cone, the top of which will be at the extremity of the tube. This experiment may be ftopped and renewed, almoft inftantly, at the word of command.

This Recreation may be diverfified by having one of thofe fountains that are made by condenfed air, as will be defcribed under the article of Hydraulics : the fountain is to be infulated, when it will pour forth one ftream only, but on being electrified, that one ftream will be divided in-

E 3   to

to a thoufand, and difperfed over a large fpace of ground. You may here command either the fingle, or the divided ftream, at pleafure, by only laying your finger on the arch or taking it off. The ftreams from both thefe fountains will appear quite luminous in the dark.

R E C R E A T I O N VI.

The magic picture.

HAVE a large print, fuppofe of the king, with a frame and glafs*. Cut a pannel out of the print at about two inches from the frame all round : with thin pafte, or gum water, fix the border that is cut off, on the infide of the glafs, preffing it fmooth and clofe, then fill up the vacancy, by covering the glafs well with leaf gold, or thin tin-foil, fo that it may lie clofe. Cover likewife the inner

---

* This experiment was invented by Mr. Kinnerfley, the author of many other improvements in electricity.

edge

edge of the bottom part of the back of the frame with the same tin-foil, and make a communication between that and the tin-foil in the middle of the glafs; then put in the board, and that fide is finifhed. Turn up the glafs and cover the forefide with tin-foil, exactly over that on the back-fide, and when it is dry, pafte over it the pannel of the print that was cut out, obferving to bring the correfponding parts of the border and the pannel together, fo that the picture will appear as at firft, only part of it behind the glafs, and part before. Laftly, hold the print horizontally by the top, and place a little moveable gilt crown on the king's head *.

Now if the tin-foil on both fides of the glafs be moderately electrified, and another perfon take hold of the bottom of the frame with one hand, fo that his fingers

* If you have not the figure of a crown, a guinea or fhilling will fhew the experiment equally well.

E 4

touch

touch the tin–foil, and with the other hand endeavour to take off the crown, he will receive a very fmart blow, and fail in the attempt. The operator who holds the frame by the upper end, where there is no tin–foil, feels nothing of the fhock, and can touch the face of the king without danger, which he pretends to be a teft of his loyalty. When a ring of perfons take a fhock among them, the experiment is called the confpirators.

R E C R E A T I O N   VII.

The Tantalian cup.

PLACE a cup or pot, of any fort of metal, on a ftool of baked wood, or a cake of wax. Fill it to the brim with any fort of liquor : let it communicate with the branch by a fmall chain, and when it is moderately electrified, defire a perfon to tafte the liquor, without touch-ing the cup with his hands, and he will immediately receive a fhock at his lips ;
which,

which, however, fhould not be very ftrong.

The motion of the wheel being ftopped, you offer to tafte the liquor yourfelf, and defire the reft of the company to tafte it likewife, which they will do without any inconvenience. You then give the fignal to the operator, and while you are amufing the company with difcourfe, the cup is again charged, and you defire the fame perfon a fecond time to tafte the liquor, when, to the no fmall diverfion of the company, he will receive a fecond fhock.

RECREATION VIII.

The circular chimes.

LET a small upright shaft of wood pass, at right angles, through a thin round board, of about twelve inches diameter, and let the shaft turn on a sharp point of iron fixed in the lower end; while a strong wire in the upper end, passing through a small hole in a thin brass plate, keeps the shaft truly vertical. About 30 radii, of equal length, made of sash glass, cut in narrow slips, are to issue horizontally from the circumference of the board; the ends most distant from the center being about four inches asunder, and on the end of every one of them is fixed a brass thimble. If a wire fixed to either of the links at F or H, while the other end of that chain communicates with the wire of a bottle electrified in the common way, be brought near the circumference of the the wheel, it will attract the nearest thimble,

ble, and fo put the wheel in motion. That thimble, in paffing by, receives a fpark, and being thereby electrified, is repelled, and fo driven forward, while a fecond thimble, being attracted, approaches the wire, receives a fpark, and is driven after the firft, and fo on, till the wheel has gone once round ; when the thimbles be-fore electrified approaching the wire, in-ftead of being attracted as they were at firft, they are repelled, and the motion prefently ceafes.

But if a wire communicating with the other chain, that is connected with another bottle charged through the coating, be brought near the fame wheel, it will attract the thimble repelled by the firft, and there-by double the force that carries the wheel round ; and not only taking out the fire that had been communicated by the thim-bles to the firft wire, but even robbing them of their natural quantity ; inftead of being repelled when they come again
toward

toward the firſt wire, they are more ſtrongly attracted; ſo that the wheel mends its pace, till it goes with great rapidity, twelve or fifteen rounds in a minute, and with ſuch ſtrength, that the weight of four or five pounds, when laid on it, does not viſibly retard its motion *.

* This part of the machine is ſometimes called an electrical jack : for if a large fowl be ſpitted on the upper ſhaft, it will be carried round with a motion fit for roaſting ; and it appears from one of Dr. Franklin's letters, that it has been actually applied to this purpoſe. " In the year 1748, the hot weather coming on, when electrical experiments were not ſo agreeable, we put an end to them for that ſeaſon, ſays the Doctor, ſomewhat humourouſly, in a party of pleaſure on the banks of the Skuylkil. Firſt, ſpirits were fired by a ſpark ſent from ſide to ſide through the river, without any other conductor than the water. A turkey was killed for our dinner by an electrical ſhock, and roaſted by the electrical jack, before a fire kindled by the electrical bottle ; and the healths of all the famous electricians in England, Holland, France, and Germany, were drank in electrified bumpers, under a diſcharge of guns from the electrical battery." Franklin's Letters, p. 35.

Now

Now if a radius of baked wood, of about eight inches, be fixed in the upper fhaft, and a number of fmall bells, correfponding to the notes of a tune, be placed on pillars, and fixed in two femicircular ftands, at a proper diftance from the thimbles, when the wheel turns round the radius will ftrike againft the bells, and confequently play the tune; and as the celerity of the wheels is continually altering, fo will be the time, or duration of the notes. It is to be obferved, that the two femicircles in which the bells are fixed, muft not be brought within reach of the radius till the wheel has acquired a confiderable velocity, for otherwife they will at leaft check, if not totally ftop, its motion. If the ftroke of the wooden radius do not give a tone fufficiently acute, a piece of folid glafs may be fixed to the end of it.

If a greater variety of tones is required there may be two fets of bells, one for the treble

treble and the other for the bafe. The bells may likewife be made to take out of the ftand, fo as to perform different tunes by being placed in different pofitions.

R E C R E A T I O N IX.

The felf-moving wheel.

THIS wheel, though conftructed on the fame principles with the foregoing, appears ftill more furprifing. It is formed of a thin round plate of window-glafs, 17 inches diameter, well gilt on both fides, all but two inches next the edge. Two fmall hemifpheres of wood are then fixed with cement to the middle of the upper and under fides, centrally oppofite, and in each of them a thick ftrong wire, eight or ten inches long, which together make the axis of the wheel. It turns horizontally, on a point at the lower end of its axis, which refts on a bit of brafs, cemented within a glafs falt-cellar. The upper end of its axis paffes through

7   a hole

a hole in a thin brafs plate, cemented to a long and ftrong piece of glafs, which keeps it fix or eight inches diftant from any non-electric, and has a fmall ball of wax or metal on the top, to keep in the fire.

In a circle on the table which fupports the wheel, are fixed twelve fmall pillars of glafs, at about eleven inches diftance, with a thimble on the top of each. On the edge of the wheel is a fmall leaden bullet, communicating by a wire with the gilding of the upper furface of the wheel ; and about fix inches from it is another bullet, communicating, in like manner, with the under furface. When the wheel is to be charged by the upper furface, a communication muft be made from the under furface to the table.

When it is well charged it begins to move. The bullet neareft to a pillar moves towards the thimble on that pillar, and passing

passing by, electrifies it, and then pushes itself from it. The succeeding bullet, which communicates with the other surface of the glass, more strongly attracts that thimble, on account of its being electrified before by the other bullet, and thus the wheel increases its motion, till it is regulated by the resistance of the air. It will go half an hour, and make, one minute with another, 20 turns in a minuet, which is 600 turns in the whole. The bullet of the upper surface gives in each turn 12 sparks to the thimbles, which makes 7200 sparks; and the bullet of the under surface receives as many from the thimbles, those bullets moving in the same time 2500 feet. The thimbles are well fixed, and in so exact a circle, that the bullets may pass within a very small distance of them.

If instead of two bullets, you put eight, four communicating with the upper surface,

face, and four with the under furface, placed alternately, (which eight, at about fix inches diftance, complete the circumference) the force and celerity will be greatly increafed; the wheel making 50 turns in a minute; but then it will not continue fo long in motion.

RECREATION X.

The magician's chace.

ON the top of a finely pointed wire, rifing perpendicularly from the conductor, let another wire, fharpened at each end, be made to move freely, as on a center. If it be well balanced, and the points be bent horizontally, in oppofite directions, it will, when electrified, turn very fwiftly round, by the re-action of the air againft the current which flows from off the points. Thefe points may be nearly concealed, and the figures of men and horfes, with hounds and a hare or fox,

VOL. III.   F   may

may be placed upon the wires, fo as to turn round with them, when they will look as if the one purfued the other *. If the number of wires proceeding from the fame center be increafed, and a ftill greater variety of figures be put upon them, the chace muft be more diverfified and enter-taining. If the wire which fupports the figures have another wire finely pointed, rifing from its center, a fecond fet of wires, furnifhed with another fort of figures, may be made to revolve above the for-mer, and either in the fame or the con-trary direction, as the operator fhall think fit.

If fuch a wire, pointed at each end, and the ends bent in oppofite directions, be furnifhed, like a dipping needle, with a fmall axis fixed in its middle, at right an-

* This is alfo an invention of Mr. Kinnerfly, and is called by him, when the figures of horfes only are ufed, the electrical horfe-race.

gles

gles with the bending of the points, and
the fame be placed between two infulated
wire ftrings, near and parallel to each
other, fo that it may turn on its axis
freely upon and between them, it will,
when electrified, have a progreffive as
well as circular motion, from one end
of the wires that fupport it to the other;
and this even up a confiderable afcent.

R E C R E A T I O N XI.

The planetarium.

FROM the branch fufpend fix concentric hoops of metal, at different diftances from each other; and under them,
on a ftand, place a metal plate, at the
diftance of about half an inch.   Then
place upon the plate, within each hoop,
and near to it, a round glafs bubble, blown
very light; thefe bubbles and the diftances
between the hoops fhould correfpond to
the different diameters of the planets, and
F 2   thofe

thofe of their orbits ; but as that cannot be on account of the vaft difproportion between them, it muft fuffice here to make a difference that bears fome relation to them.

Now the hoops being electrified, the bubbles placed upon the plate, near the hoops, will be immediately attracted by them ; in confequence of which, that part of a bubble which touches a hoop will acquire fome electric virtue, and be repelled : the electricity not being diffufed over the whole furface of the glafs, another part of the furface will be attracted, while the former goes to difcharge its electricity upon the plate. This will produce a revolution of the bubble quite round the hoop, as long as the electrification is continued, and will be either way, juft as the bubble happens to fet out, or is driven by the operator. A ball hung over the center of all the hoops will ferve to reprefent

prefent the fun, in the center, of its fyf-
tem. If the room be darkened the feveral glafs balls will appear beautifully illuminated. This experiment affords a remarkable inftance of electric attraction and
repulfion.

RECREATION XII.

The incendiaries.

LET a perfon ftand upon a ftool made
of baked wood, or upon a cake of
wax, and hold a chain communicating with
the branch. Upon turning the wheel he
will foon become electrified; his whole
body, in reality, making a part of the
prime conductor, and will exhibit the
fame appearances; emitting fparks where-
ever he is touched by any perfon ftanding
on the floor. If the prime conductor be
very large, the fparks may be rather pain-
ful than agreeable; but if it be fmall, the
electrification moderate, and none of the

F 3

com-

company touch the eyes, or the more tender parts of the face, the experiment is diverting enough to all parties.

Many of the preceding experiments may also be performed to advantage by a perfon standing upon the ftool as above, and holding in his hand what was directed to be faftened to the prime conductor. If he hold a large plumy feather in his hand, it is very pleafing to obferve how it becomes turgid, its fibres extending themfelves in all directions from the rib; and how it fhrinks, like the fenfitive plants, when any unelectrified body touches it; when the point of a needle is prefented to it, or to the prime conductor with which he is connected.

If a difh, containing fpirits of wine made warm, be brought to the electrified perfon, and he be directed to put his finger,

finger, or a rod of iron into it, the spirit will be immediately in a blaze; and if there be a wick or thread in the spirit, that communicates with a train of gun-powder, he may be made to blow up a ma-gazine, or set a city on fire with a piece of cold iron ; and at the same time know no-thing of what he is about.

A recreation of this sort may be per-formed by several persons, that all stand upon insulated stools, and many diverting circumstances may be added to those here mentioned. Care should be taken that the floor on which the stools stand be free from dust, but it is most eligible to have a large smooth board for that purpose.

RECRE-

RECREATION XIII.

The inconceivable shock.

PUT into a person's hand a wire that is fixed on to the hook that comes from the chain which communicates with one side of the battery, and in his other hand put a wire with a hook at the end of it, which you direct him to fix on to the hook that comes from the other chain, which when he attempts he will instantly receive a shock through his body, without being able to guess from whence it proceeds. The shock will be in proportion to the number of jars that are charged ; but it is remarkable, that a small shock gives a much more pungent sensation in passing through the body, than one that is large *.

* The shock may be made to pass through any particular part of the body, without much affecting the rest, if that part, and no other, be brought into the circuit through which the fire must pass from one side of the jar or battery to the other.

This

This recreation may be diverſified, and rendered ſtill more entertaining, by concealing the chain that communicates with that which comes from the outſide of the battery, under a carpet, and placing the wire that communicates with the chain which comes from the inſide, in ſuch manner that a perſon ſhall put his hand upon it without ſuſpicion, at the ſame time that his feet are upon the other wire. Many other methods of giving a ſhock by ſurprize may be eaſily contrived ; but great care ſhould be taken that theſe ſhocks be not too ſtrong, and that they be not given to all perſons indiſcriminately.

When a ſingle perſon receives a ſhock, the company is diverted at his ſole expence ; but all contribute their ſhare to the entertainment, and all partake of it alike, when the whole company forms a circle, by joining their hands, and when the operator directs the perſon who is at one extremity of the circle, to hold the chain

6

chain which communicates with the coat
ing, while he who is at the other extremity
of the circle touches the other chain or
wire. All the perfons who form this
circuit being ftruck at the fame time, and
with the fame degree of force, it is often
very pleafant to fee them all ftart at
the fame moment, to hear them com-
pare their fenfations, and obferve the very
different accounts they give *.

This experiment may be agreeably varied, if the operator, inftead of making
the company join hands, direct them to
tread on each other's toes, or lay their
hands on each other's heads. If in the
latter cafe the whole company fhould be
ftruck to the ground, as it once happen-

* M. Monnier of Paris is faid to have communicated this fhock through a line of men, and
other conductors, of 900 toifes, that is, more than
an Englifh mile ; and Abbé Nollet performed the
fame experiment upon 200 perfons, ranged in two
parallel ranks.

ed

ed when Dr. Franklin gave the shock to
six very stout men, the inconvenience a-
rising from it will be very little : the
company that was struck in this manner neither heard nor felt the stroke, and
immediately got up again, without knowing what had happened. This stroke
was given with two large jars, each of the
measure of about six gallons, but not fully
charged.

RECREATION XIV.

Magical explosions.

WE have shown in a preceding recreation how gunpowder may be
fired by the intervention of spirits, but
there is another method, more simple and
expeditious, which we shall here describe.
Make up gunpowder in the form of a
small cartridge, in each end of which put a
blunt wire, so that the ends within the
cartridge may be about half an inch distant
from

from each other, then joining the chain that comes from one side of the battery to one of the wires at the end of the cartridge, bring the chain that comes from the other side of the battery, to the wire at the other end, when the shock will instantly pass through the powder, and set it on fire.

By a similar method fine brass or iron wire may be melted; for the explosion will pass from one chain to the other, through the wire, which will be first red hot, and then melt into round drops *. A battery of 35 jars has entirely destroyed fine brass wire, of the 330th part of an inch in diameter, so that no particle of it could be found after the explosion. At the moment of the stroke, a great number of

* The power of a battery to melt wire is different at different distances. Dr. Priestley found that he could melt nine inches of small iron wire at the distance of 15 yards, but at 20 yards distance he could only make six inches red hot.

sparks,

sparks, like those from a flint and steel, flew upward and laterally from the place where the wire was laid, and lost their light, in the day, at the distance of about two or three inches *.

A stroke from a common jar will easily strike a hole through a thick cover of a book, or many folds of paper, leaving a remarkable bur or prominence on both sides, as if the fire had darted both ways from the center.

* The late Mr. Canton, by whose ingenuity and industry this branch of philosophy received very great improvement, clearly proved, that pure gold and silver might be calcined by the electric explosion, and be converted into numberless globules of glass, some of which were transparent, and others tinged with a great variety of colours.

RECRE-

RATIONAL

RECREATION XV.

The prismatic colours *.

TO the ends of each of the chains that come from the battery, fix an iron wire, and between thofe wires place a plate of tin, of about three inches fquare, and polifhed on one fide †, in a perpendicular direction. The wire next the polifhed fide fhould be finely pointed, and brought very near the furface of the plate.

By repeating the explofions of the battery, there will firft appear a dufky red,

---

* This difcovery was made by Dr. Prieftley, and ferves to confirm the Newtonian doctrine of the difference of colours in bodies arifing from the different denfities of the fine plates that compofe their furfaces.

† The polifh is not neceffary, but the colours appear more beautiful than on a rough furface. This experiment may be made equally well with the other metals, as gold, filver, copper, brafs, iron, or lead.

about

about the edge of the central fpot; prefently after, generally after four or five
ftrokes, there appears a circular fpace, vifible only in an oblique pofition to the
light, and looking like a fhade on the
plate: this expands very little during the
whole courfe of the explofions. After
a few more difcharges, the fecond circular fpace is marked, by another fhade
beyond the firft, of one-eighth or one-
tenth of an inch in width, which never
changes its appearance after any number
of explofions. All the colours make
their firft appearance about the edge of
the circular fpot; more explofions make
them expand toward the extremity of the
fpace firft marked out; while others
fucceed in their place, till after 30 or 40
explofions, three diftinct rings appear,
each confifting of all the colours in the
prifm or rainbow.

It makes no difference whether the
electricity iffue from the pointed wire

7 upon

upon the plate, or from the plate upon the pointed wire, the furface oppofite the point being marked exactly the fame in both cafes. The points themfelves, from which the fire iffues, or at which it enters, are coloured for about half an inch to a confiderable degree, and the colours are repeated, as on the plate.

The innermoft, that is, the laft formed colours, on the plate, are always the moft vivid, and thofe rings are alfo clofer to each other than the reft. Thefe colours may be brufhed with a feather or the finger, without injury, but they are eafily peeled off by the nail, or any thing that is fharp.

RECRE-

RECREATION XVI.

The artificial earthquake.

IN the middle of a large bafon of water place a round wet board : this board reprefents the earth, and the water the fea. On the board erect an edifice, compofed of feveral feparate pieces, which may reprefent a church, a caftle, a palace, or if you pleafe all of them.

Then placing a wire that communicates with the two chains of the battery, fo that it may pafs over the board and the furface of the water, upon making the explofion the water will become agitated, as in an earthquake, and the board moving up and down, will overturn the ftructures it fupports ; at the fame time that the caufe of this commotion is totally concealed.

This

This experiment likewise was invented by Dr. Priestley, and, when well executed, cannot fail to give great surprize as well as entertainment.

RECREATION XVII.

*The electrical kite *.*

TAKE a large thin silk handkerchief, and extend it, by fastening the four corners to two slight strips of cedar. The handkerchief thus prepared and accommodated with a tail, loop, and string, will rise in the air as a common paper kite. To the top of the upright stick of the cross is to be fixed a pretty sharp-pointed wire, rising a foot or more above the wood. To the end of the twine next the hand is to be tied a silk ribband, and where the twine and silk join, a key or tin tube may be fastened.

* This is an invention of Dr. Franklin.

This

This kite is to be raifed when a thunder guft appears to be coming on, and as foon as the thunder clouds come over the kite, the pointed wire will draw the electricity from them, and the kite, with all the twine, will be electrified, the lofe filaments of the twine will ftand out every way, and be attracted by the finger.   When the rain has wetted the kite and twine, fo that it cannot conduct the electric fire freely, it will ftream out plentifully from the key, on the approach of a man's knuckle.   At this key a phial may be charged, and from the electric fire thus obtained, fpirits may be kindled, and all the other experiments performed.

The greateft quantity of electricity that was ever brought from the clouds by an apparatus, was by M. de Romas, of Nerac, in the fouth of France.   This gentleman was the firft who made ufe of a wire inter—woven in the hempen cord of an electric kite, which was feven feet and a half high,

G 2   and

and three feet wide, fo that it contained 18 fquare feet of furface. This cord was found to conduct the electricity of the clouds more powerfully than a hempen cord, even though it was wetted; and being terminated by a cord of dry filk, it enabled the obferver (by a proper management of his apparatus) to make whatever experiments he thought proper, without danger.

By the help of this kite, on the 7th of June, 1753, about one in the afternoon, when it was raifed 550 feet from the ground, and had taken 780 feet of ftring, making an angle of near 45 degrees with the horizon, he drew fparks from his conductor three inches long, and a quarter of an inch thick, the fnapping of which was heard 200 paces. While he was taking thefe fparks, he felt, as it were, a fort of cobweb on his face, though he was more than three feet from the ftring of the

* That is, being the half way between the horizon and the point directly over the fpectator's head.

kite :

kite : after which he did not think it safe to stand so near, and called aloud to all the company to retire, as he did himself about two feet.

Thinking himself now secure enough, and not being incommoded by any body very near him, he took notice of what paffed among the clouds that were immediately over the kite. There was no appearance of lightning there, or any where elfe, nor fcarce the leaft noife of thunder, and no rain at all. There was a pretty ftrong wind at weft, which raifed the kite at leaft 100 feet higher than in any other experiment. Cafting his eyes afterwards on the tin tube faftened to the ftring of the kite, and about three feet from the ground, he faw three ftraws, one of which was about a foot long, a fecond four or five inches, and the third three or four inches, all ftanding erect, and performing a circular dance, like puppets, under the tin tube, without touching each other.

G 3 This

This little fpectacle, with which feveral of the company were much delighted, lafted about a quarter of an hour; after which fome drops of rain falling, he again perceived the fenfation of the cobweb on his face, and at the fame time heard a continual ruftling noife, like that of a fmall forge bellows. This was a further warning of the increafe of electricity, and from the firft inftant Mr. De Romas perceived the dancing ftraws, he thought it not advifeable to take any more fparks, even with all his precautions; and he again intreated the company to retire to a ftill greater diftance.

Immediately after this came on the laft act of the entertainment, which M. De Romas acknowledges made him tremble. The longeft ftraw was attracted by the tin tube, upon which there followed three explofions, the found of which greatly refembled that of thunder. Some of the company compared it to the explofion of rockets,

rockets, and others to the violent craſhing of large earthen jars againſt a pavement. It is certain that it was heard into the heart of the city, notwithſtanding the various noiſes there.

The fire that was ſeen at the inſtant of explosion had the ſhape of a ſpindle, eight inches long, and five lines in diameter. But the moſt aſtoniſhing and diverting circumſtance was produced by the ſtraw, which had occaſioned the exploſion, following the ſtring of the kite. Some of the company ſaw it at 45 or 50 fathoms diſtance, attracted and repelled alternately, with this remarkable circumſtance, that every time it was attracted by the ſtring, flaſhes of fire were ſeen, and cracks were heard, though not ſo loud as at the time of the former exploſion.

It is remarkable, that from the time of the exploſion, to the end of the experiment, no lightning at all was ſeen, and ſcarce any

any thunder heard. A fmell of fulphur was perceived, much like that of the luminous electric effluvia iffuing from the end of an electrified bar of metal. Round the ftring appeared a luminous cylinder of light, three or four inches in diameter ; and as this was in the day time, M. de Romas did not queftion but that if it had been in the night, the electric atmofphere would have appeared to be four or five feet in diameter. An end was put to thefe remarkable experiments, by the wind's fhifting to the eaft, and rain, mixed with hail, coming on in great plenty *.

* The quantity of electric matter brought by this kite from the clouds at another time is really aftonifhing. Auguft 26, 1756, the ftreams of fire iffuing from it were obferved to be an inch thick; and ten feet long. Thefe amazing flafhes of lightning, whofe report was equal to that of a piftol, and whofe effect, had any of them ftruck on buildings, or animal bodies, would perhaps have been equally deftructive with any mentioned in hiftory, were fafely conducted by the cord of the kite, to a non-electric body placed near it.

As

As the foregoing account might deter some perfons from attempting this very entertaining experiment, efpecially when there is the appearance of an approaching thunder-ftorm, we fhall here add an apparatus, invented by Dr. Prieftley, and with which he thinks there can be no great danger in any thunder-ftorm.

Let the ftring A, of a kite (Plate IV. Fig. 4.) be wound upon a reel B, going through a flit in a flat board, faftened at the top of it; by which more or lefs of the ftring may be let out at pleafure.   Let the reel be fixed to the top of a tin or copper funnel C, and from the funnel let a metal rod D, with a large knob, be projected, to ferve as a conductor.   This funnel and reel muft be fupported by a ftaff E, the upper end of which, at leaft, muft be well baked, and the lower end may be made fharp, to thruft into the ground, when the kite is well raifed.

The

...The safety of this apparatus depends on the chain F, faftened to the ftaff by a hook a little below the funnel, and dragging on the ground : for the redundant lightning will ftrike from the funnel to the chain, and fo be conducted as far as is defired, without touching the perfon who holds the ftaff.

Sparks may be taken from the conductor of this apparatus, with all fafety, by means of a fmall rod of baked wood A, Fig. 4. furnifhed with a fmall funnel B, a brafe rod C, and a chain connected with it; for the lightning which ftrikes the rod, will pafs by the funnel and the chain, without touching the perfon who holds the rod.

R E C R E-

PLATE IV.

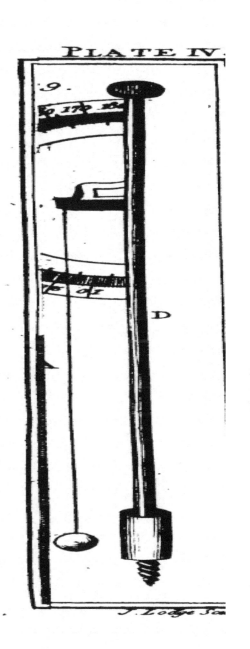

RECREATIONS IN THE DARK CHAMBER.

To exhibit a great number of pleaſing and
ſurpriſing recreations in the dark, as
well as in the light, is the peculiar property of electricity : for though there
are many beautiful experiments performed in the camera obſcura, it is ſtill
by the aid of the ſun's rays, or thoſe of
a candle or lamp : whereas the electric
apparatus contains within itſelf thoſe
particles of fire by which theſe recreations are performed.

RECREATION XVIII.

The miraculous luminaries.

TO perform this recreation it is necef-
ſary to be provided with a quantity
of the following phoſphorus. Calcine
common oyſter-ſhells, by burning them
in the fire for about half an hour ;
then beat them into powder, of the cleareſt
of

of which take three parts, and of flowers of sulphur one part, and put the mixture into a crucible about one inch and a half deep. Let it burn in a strong open fire, for a full hour; when cool turn it out, and break it into several pieces, and taking those pieces into a dark place, scrape off the brightest parts for use, which, when good, will be a white powder.

Then take a circular board of three or four feet diameter, on the center of which draw the figure of the half moon, of three or four inches diameter, and round it, at different distances, draw a number of stars, of different magnitudes. On each of these figures fix the phosphorus just mentioned, to the thickness of about a quarter of an inch. The board being thus prepared, you must have ready a number of charged jars, or phials, and by discharging one of them, at the distance of about an inch, over each figure, it will become illuminated. The light of the crescent will be so strong

at

at firſt, that you may diſtinguiſh by it the figures on the dial of a watch. Round the board let there be placed a rim or hoop, and over that, at a ſufficient diſtance from the figures, draw a curtain.

The board thus prepared is to be brought into the darkened room, and placed, by hooks, againſt the ceiling. The curtain is then to be drawn back, and the moon and ſtars will appear as emerging from behind a cloud, and will continue to ſhine for half an hour; the light, however, growing continually more faint.

Previous to the performing the following recreation, it will be neceſſary to have a globe and cuſhion placed on the middle of the table, which muſt communicate, by a ſtring that goes through the partition, with the wheel in the other room.

RECRE-

RECREATION XIX.

The globular fires.

LET the room, and all the parts of the apparatus, be made very dry, and let the globe be ftrongly excited, fo that the electricity may be very vigorous; the fire will then be feen to dart from the cufhion toward the wire of the conductor. Sometimes thefe lucid rays (which are in part vifible in day-light) will make the circuit of half the globe, and reach the wires ; and they will frequently come in a confiderable number, at the fame time, from different parts of the cufhion, and reach within an inch or two of the wires. The noife attending this beautiful phenomenon exactly refembles the crackling of bay leaves in the fire. Thefe lucid arches have frequently radiant points, often four or five in different parts of the fame arch. Thefe radiant points are intenfely bright,

and

and appear very beautiful. It is peculiarly pleasing to observe the circles of fire rise from those parts of the cushion, where the amalgam or moisture has been put, or which have been lately scraped. Single points on the rubber will then appear intensely bright, and for a long time together will seem to pour out continual torrents of flame. If one part of the rubber be pressed closer than another, the circles will issue from that part more frequently than from any other.

When the conductor is taken quite away, circles of fire will appear on both sides the rubber, which will sometimes meet, and completely encircle the globe. If in that state a finger be brought within half an inch of the globe, it is sure to be struck very smartly; and there will often be a complete arch of fire from it to the rubber, though it be almost quite round the globe.

If

If all the air be exhaufted from the globe, the electricity will be found to act wholly within it, where it will appear in the form of a cloud or flame of reddifh or purple-coloured light, filling the whole interior fpace of the globe *.

RECREATION XX.

The luminous fhower.

ON the plate at *n*, Plate II. put a number of feeds of any kind; or grains of fand, or a quantity of brafs duft. The conductor being ftrongly electrified, thofe light particles will be attracted and repelled by the plate *o*, fufpended from the conductor, with amazing rapidity, fo as to exhibit a perfect luminous fhower.

* When this recreation is finifhed the globe and rubber muft be taken away, that they may not incommode the apparatus of the following experiments.

Another

Another method of reprefenting luminous rain, is by a fpunge that has been
immerfed in water. When this fpunge
is firft hung to the conductor, the water
will drop from it very flowly; but when
it is electrified, the drops will fall very
faft, and will appear like globules of fire,
illuminating the bafon into which they
fall.

RECREATION XXI.

The illuminated vacuum.

TAKE a tall receiver that is very dry,
and through the top of it fix, with
cement, a wire, not very acutely pointed.
Then exhauft the receiver, and prefent the
knob of the wire to the conductor, and
every fpark will pafs through the vacuum,
in a broad ftream of light, vifible through
the whole length of the receiver, how tall
foever it be. This ftream often divides
itfelf into a variety of beautiful rivulets,
which are continually changing their

VOL. III.   H   courfe,

courfe, uniting and dividing again in a moft pleafing manner. If a jar be difcharged through this vacuum, it gives the appearance of a very denfe body of fire, darting directly through the center of the vacuum, withont ever touching the fides : whereas, when a fingle fpark paffes through, it generally goes more or lefs to the fide, and a finger put to the outfide of the glafs, will draw it wherever a perfon pleafe. If the veffel be grafped by both hands, every fpark is felt, like the pulfation of a large artery, and all the fire makes towards the hands. This pulfation is felt at fome diftance from the receiver, and a light is feen between the hands and the glafs.

All this while the pointed wire is fuppofed to be electrified pofitively; if it be electrified negatively, the appearance is remarkably different. Inftead of ftreams of fire, nothing is feen but one uniform luminous appearance, like a white cloud, or the

the milky way in a clear ftar-light night. It feldom reaches the whole length of the veffel, but generally appears only at the end of the wire, like a lucid ball.

If in the neck of a tall receiver a fmall phial be inferted, fo that the external fur-face of the glafs may be expofed to the vacuum, it will produce a very beautiful appearance. The phial muft be coated on the infide, and while it is charging, at every fpark taken from the conductor into the infide, a flafh of light is feen to dart, at the fame time, from every part of the external furface of the phial, fo as to quite fill the receiver. Upon making the difcharge, the light is feen to return in a much clofer body, the whole coming out at once.

RE-

R E C R E A T I O N XXII.

The luminous cylinder *.

PROVIDE a glafs cylinder three feet long and three inches diameter : near the bottom of it fix a brafs plate, and have another brafs plate fo contrived that you may let it down the cylinder, and bring it as near the firft plate as you defire. Let this cylinder be exhaufted and infulated, and when the upper part is electrified, the electric matter will pafs from one plate to the other, when they are at the greateft diftance from each other the cylinder will admit. The brafs plate at the bottom of the cylinder will moreover be as ftrongly electrified, as if it was connected by a wire with the prime conductor.

The electric matter in its paffage thro' this vacuum is faid to produce a delightful

* This is an invention of Dr. Watfon.

fpec–

spectacle ; not making, as in the open air, small brushes or pencils of rays, an inch or two in length, but coruscations of the whole length of the tube, and of a bright silver hue. These do not immediately diverge, as in the open air, but frequently form a base that is apparently flat, dividing themselves into less and less ramifications, and very much resemble the most lively coruscations of the aurora borealis.

RECREATION XXIII.

The magical constellations.

AS the moon and stars in the zenith will become dull during the time of performing the preceding recreations, it will be proper to draw the curtain gently before them, that it may seem as if a cloud came slowly over them ; and then the operator may, by his magical power, light up other constellations. In order to which,

he

he muſt provide a large board, on which
let him mark the ſtars that are in two or
more conſtellations, which are contiguous
and viſible in the northern hemiſphere, as
Taurus, Gemini, &e.

To repreſent theſe ſtars, let there be a
hole on each ſide of the ſpot that is marked for a ſtar, at about a quarter of an inch
diſtant from each other, and let the extremities of two wires, neatly rounded,
come through theſe holes, and be brought
near together, exactly over the mark.
Theſe wires ſhould be of different ſizes,
that they may the better repreſent the different magnitudes of the ſtars.

The other ends of the wires muſt be
ſo diſpoſed, that they may all receive a
ſpark from the conductor at the ſame
time, and the ſtars will then be all luminous at the ſame inſtant. Theſe ſtars
are not evaneſcent, like thoſe made by
the phoſphorus, but will continue with
                                                    equal

equal fplendor as long as the motion of the wheel is continued. After the fame manner any cypher, or the outlines of a drawing may be exhibited.

RECREATION XXIV.

The luminous charaɛters *.

PROVIDE a board about four inches wide, as A B, (Plate III. Fig. 1.) and of what length you pleafe. On this board place ten or twelve rows of tin-foil, at about half an inch diftance from each other, and that all communicate together. From thefe lines are to be cut out the charaɛters you intend to reprefent ; obferving that the ends of the tin-foil where it is cut, fhould not be ftrait, but pointed as in the figure.

At the beginning of the tin-foil there muft be a brafs knob C, which being brought

---

* This is an invention of Mr. Henly, the author of the graduated eleɛtrometer defcribed in the appaꞔatus.

H 4

to

to the conductor, receives the electricity and conveys it to the tin-foil, over which it would run imperceptibly, were there no breaks in the lines, but being there interrupted, it jumps from one point to the other, making at the same time a lucid spot, by which the characters are formed, and will continue as long as the wheel is in motion. If at the same time the knob is applied to the conductor, the operator place his finger against the other end of the uppermost line of the tin-foil, and draw it flowly down, over the ends of the other lines, it will feem as if the characters were formed by the motion of his hand.

This experiment may be made by the discharge of a jar or phial, but it will then be of a short continuance. By this method also the conftellations, or the outlines of a drawing, &c. may be reprefented.

R E-

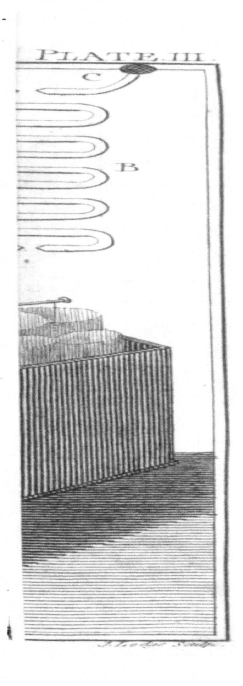

PLATE III.

RECREATION XXV.

Prismatic illuminations *.

TAKE a glaſs veſſel about a foot long and eight inches diameter, open at both ends; and let one of its ends be cloſed by a braſs ferule, which is to conſtitute one of the centers on which it is to turn : the other end muſt be cloſed with a metal plate. In the center of the plate let there be a ſquare ſtem, which is to be applied to the arbor of a lathe, by which the globe is to be turned round. On one ſide of this laſt plate muſt be fixed a cork, by means of which the glaſs is ſcrewed upon the air-pump.

Upon rarefying the air within the glaſs about 500 times, and afterwards turning

* This experiment was firſt made by Mr. Smeaton, the inventor of the new air-pump.

7   the

the glafs in the lathe, and rubbing it at the fame time with the hand, a confiderable quantity of lambent flame, variegated with all the colours of the rainbow, will appear within the glafs, under the hand. This light is perpetually changing colour under the hand, but in every other refpect is pretty fteady.

When a little air is let into the glafs, the light appears more vivid, and in greater quantity, but is not fo fteady, for it will frequently break out into a kind of coruf-cation, like lightning, and fly all over the interior part of the glafs. When a little more air is let in, the flafhing is continual, and ftreams of bluifh light feem to iffue from under the hand, within the glafs, in a thoufand forms, with great rapidity, and appear like a cafcade of fire. Sometimes it is feen to fhoot out into the form of trees, mofs, &c.

When

When more air is let in, the quantity of light is diminifhed, and the ftreams that compofe the flafhes narrower. The glafs now requires greater velocity, and harder friction. Thefe circumftances will increafe as ftill more air is let in, fo that by the time the glafs is one-third full of air, the corufcations quite vanifh, and a much fmaller quantity of light appears, partly within and partly without the glafs. When all the air is let in, the light appears wholly without the glafs, and much lefs in quantity than when the glafs is only in part exhaufted.

RECRE-

RECREATION   XXVI.

The aurora borealis *.

MAKE a Torricellian vacuum in a glafs tube, about three feet long, and feal it hermetically †: it will then be always ready for ufe.' Let one end of this tube be held in the hand, and the other applied to the conductor, and immediately the whole tube will be illuminated, from end to end; and when taken from the conductor will continue luminous, without interruption, for a confiderable time, very often above a quarter of

* This is one of the inventions of that great benefactor to this fcience, Mr. Canton.

† The Torricellian vacuum is made by filling a tube with pure mercury, and then inverting it, in the fame manner as in making a barometer; for as the mercury runs out, all the fpace above will be a true vacuum. A glafs is hermetically fealed by holding the end of it in the flame of a candle till it is ready to melt, and then twifting it together with a pair of pincers.

an

an hour. If after this, it be drawn thro'
the hand either way, the light will be un-
commonly intenfe, and, without the leaft
interruption, from one hand to the other,
even to its whole length. After this operation, which difcharges it in a great meafure, it will ftill flafh at intervals, though
it be held only at one extremity, and quite
ftill; but if it be grafped by the other hand
at the fame time, in a different place,
ftrong flafhes of light will hardly ever fail
to dart from one end to the other; and this
will continue 24 hours, and perhaps much
longer; without frefh excitation. Small
and long glafs tubes exhaufted of air, and
bent in many irregular crooks and angles,
will, when properly electrified, beautifully
reprefent flafhes of lightning.

RECREATION XXVII.

The circulating lamps.

AFTER keeping the company thus long in the dark, it will be proper to illuminate the room before you difmifs them. In order to which, introduce the circulating wheel, mentioned in the 9th Recreation. To the upper axis of which let there be fixed a number of radii, made of baked wood, at the end of each of which muft hang a fmall globular lamp, filled with fpirits; and let that of each lamp be tinged with a different colour. The wheel, having previoufly acquired its greateft velocity, is to be placed on the table, and a chain, depending from the branch, is to dip into each lamp as it paffes by; fo that all of them will become illuminated in a very fhort time. Thefe lamps will not only enlighten the room, but by their variegated colours, and continual revolution, afford a very pleafing phenomenon.

M A G—

MAGNETISM.

MAGNETISM.

DEFINITIONS.

1. MAGNETISM is the science that explains the several properties of the attractive and repellent powers in the magnet or loadstone.

2. The magnet is a rich, heavy, iron ore, of a hard substance, a dusky grey colour, with some mixture of a reddish brown, and sparkling when broke.

3. The magnetic virtue is called the third species of attraction ; gravity being the first, and electricity the second.

4. The two ends of a magnet, when it is properly formed, are called its poles ; and when it is placed on a pivot, in just equilibrium, one end will turn toward the north, and is called its north pole, and the other end the south pole *.

* The poles of a magnet are found by holding a very fine short needle over it ; for where the

5. When the two poles of a magnet are furrounded with plates of fteel, it is faid to be armed.

6. If the end of a fmall iron bar be rubbed againft one of the poles of a magnet, it is faid to be touched, and is then called an artificial magnet.

7. If fuch a magnet be fupported on a pivot, it is called a magnetic needle; one end of it turning toward the north, and the other toward the fouth.

8. The difference between the pofition of the needle, and the exact points of north and fouth, is called its declination.

9. That end of the needle which is touched will incline toward the earth, and that is called its inclination or dipping.

poles are the needle will ftand upright, but no-where elfe. The exterior parts are then to be filed or ground off, and the two extremities which contain the poles, to be made quite fmooth.

APHORISMS.

1. The magnetic attraction is produced by effluvia emitted by the magnet, and passing from one pole to the other *.

2. One pole of a magnet will attract iron, and the other repel it, but no other body †.

* The direction of the magnetic effluvia is shown by the following experiment. Let AB, CD, (Plate V. Fig. 1.) be the poles of a magnet. Round every side lightly strew steel filings, on a sheet of white paper ; the particles of the filings will be so effected by the effluvia of the stone, as to show the course they take every way. In the middle of each pole, between A B and C D, they appear to proceed in lines nearly straight ; toward the ends they are more and more curved, till at last the lines from both sides, coinciding with each other, form numberless curves round the stone, which are nearly of a circular figure, as in the plate. This experiment seems to show that the magnetic effluvia, issuing from one pole, circulates to the other.

† The property of the magnet to attract iron has been known many ages : but those of its polar direction, and of its communicating that property to iron, was not discovered till the 14th century.

I 2

3. The

3. The magnet attracts iron as well in vacuo, as in the air.

4. The magnetic attraction will be continued through several pieces of iron placed contiguous to each other.

5. The magnetic effluvia pervades all bodies.

6. The magnetic attraction extends to a confiderable diftance *.

7. The north pole of one magnet will attract the fouth pole of another : and the fimilar poles will repel each other †.

---

* The learned Mufchenbroek made a number of experiments, with great care and affiduity, to determine the extent and progrefs of the magnetic attraction, but was never able to difcover any regular proportion between the force and diftance; but merely that the force increafed as the iron approached the magnet. Nor does there feem to be any profpect of eftablifhing the proportion of attraction to the diftance, till a method is found, if it can be found, of feparating the attracting from the repelling parts. A needle has been known to be attracted by an iron bar at the diftance of eight or ten feet.

† If a magnet be gently cut through the middle of its axis, each piece becomes a complete magnet; for

8. The end of a needle touched by the north pole of a magnet will turn fouth, and that touched by the fouth pole will turn north.

9. The declination of the magnetic needle is different in different parts of the earth, and in the fame part at different times *.

10. The inclination of the needle is not

for the parts that were contiguous become poles, aad even oppofite poles. So that the end of each piece may become a north or fouth pole according as the fection is made neareft to the north or fouth pole of the large magnet. Upon cutting a magnet longitudinally, there will be four poles, in the fame pofition as before the cutting. Sometimes a ftrong ftroke with a hammer will bring all the magnetic power from one end of a needle to the other ; fometimes make it more ftrong where it was before, and at other times totally deftroy it.

* The declination of the needle at London, in the year 1580, was 11 degrees, 15 minutes eaft. In the year 1657, there was no declination, that is, the needle ftood exactly north and fouth. At prefent, the declination is more than 20 degrees weftward.

I 3

always the same in different places, nor in the same place at different times *.

11. The strength of natural magnets differs in those of different magnitudes, but not in proportion to their magnitudes †.

---

* The inclination of the needle when it was first observed, in the year 1576, was found to be 71 degrees 50 minutes : at present it is between 74 and 75 degrees.

To prevent the dipping of the needle in the common compass, the end that is not touched is made something heavier, by which it is kept in equilibrium. Under the equator the needle has no inclination, being equally attracted by the two poles of the earth.

† The smallest magnets have generally the greatest power, in proportion to their bulk. A large magnet will seldom take up more than three or four times its own weight ; whereas a small one will frequently take up more than ten times its weight. A magnet that weighs scarce three grains, and that a gentleman wears in his ring, will take up 746 grains, or 250 times its own weight. A magnetic bar made by Mr. Canton, according to the method we shall hereafter describe, and that weighed 10 ounces 12 pennyweights, took up something more than 79 ounces ; and a flat semi-
circular

12. The strength of a natural magnet is considerably increased by its being armed *.

circular steel magnet that weighed an ounce and 13 pennyweights, lifted an iron wedge of 90 ounces.

* There are various ways of arming magnets ; the most eligible seems to be that of placing two pieces of steel against the two poles, so that they may come down below the bottom of the stone, and binding them on with one or more pieces of brass ; the two ends of the steel pieces then become the poles of the magnet. To determine the quantity of steel to be applied, try the magnet with several steel bars, and the greatest weight it takes up, with a bar on, is to be the weight of its armour.

Though an armed magnet have a great degree of force, it may be easily counteracted. If an oblong piece of iron be suspended by one of its poles, and the pole of a different denomination of a weaker and unarmed magnet be placed under the iron, it will quit the first magnet, and adhere to the other. In like manner when a needle hangs by its point to a magnet, if a common bar of iron be applied to the head of the needle, it will directly quit the magnet and adhere to the bar ; but if it hang by its head to the magnet, neither the iron, nor a weak magnet, will disengage it. Tho'

I 4 the

13. Iron acquires a magnetic power by being continually rubbed in the fame direction *.

14. Iron bars become magnetic by ftanding a long time nearly upright †.

the pole of an armed magnet have great power, yet if an iron bar of great length be placed under it, the magnet will not appear to have any force whatever.

If a magnet, by lying a long time unufed, have loft part of its power, it may fometimes be recovered. An armed magnet that weighed 14 ounces and a half, and would take up 16 times its own weight, by laying by fome years loft one-fourth part of its power. But as much weight being applied to it, as it would then take up, and being fuffered to hang to it fome weeks, it would then take up an additional quantity ; and the quantity being continually increafed, at different periods, for the fpace of two years, it would then take up more than 20 pounds ; whereas, before its virtue was impaired, it would not take up 15.

* From hence files, augurs, and fuch like tools, have always fome magnetic power.

† Therefore pokers, tongs, and other irons, that always ftand with the fame end downward, are conftantly magnetic. Some bars acquire feveral

15. The magnetic virtue may be communicated by electricity *.

16. A strong blow at the end of a short iron bar will give it a magnetic power †.

17. Fire totally destroys the power of magnets, as well natural as artificial.

veral magnetic poles, alternately north and south.

* When the electric shock is very strong it will give a polarity to needles; and sometimes it will reverse their poles.

† If such a bar, or a pair of pincers, be struck hard, or thrown forcibly aganist a stone floor, they will manifestly attract a small needle that floats upon the surface of the water in a glass,

METHOD

METHOD OF MAKING ARTIFICIAL MAGNETS*.

PROCURE a dozen bars; fix of foft fteel, each three inches long, one quarter of an inch broad, and one-twentieth of an inch thick, with two pieces of iron, each half the length of one of the bars, but of the fame breadth and thicknefs; and fix of hard fteel, each five inches and a half long, half an inch broad, and three-twentieths of an inch thick, with two pieces of iron of one half the length, but the fame breadth and thicknefs as one of the hard bars; and let all the bars be marked with a line quite round them at one end.

Then take an iron poker and tongs (Plate VI. Fig. 1.) the larger they are and

* There are various methods of making thefe magnets: this method is taken from the 47th volume of the Philofophical Tranfactions, and was invented by the late Mr. Canton; to whom the learned world is indebted for many ufeful difcoveries and improvements in magnetifm, as well as electricity.

4   the

the longer they have been ufed, the better ;
and fixing the poker upright between the
knees, hold to it, near the top, one of the
foft bars, having its marked end downward, by a piece of fewing filk, which
muft be pulled tight with the left hand,
that the bar may not flide : then grafping
the tongs with the right hand, a little below the middle, and holding them nearly
in a vertical pofition, let the bar be ftroked,
by the lower end, from the bottom to the
top, about ten times on each fide, which
will give it a magnetic power fufficient to
lift a fmall key at the marked end ; which
end, if the bar was fufpended on a point,
would turn toward the north, and is therefore called the north pole, and the un-
marked end is, for the fame reafon, called
the fouth pole of the bar.

Four of the foft bars being impregnated
after this manner, lay the other two
(Fig. 2.) parallel to each other, at the diftance of about a quarter of an inch,
between

between the two pieces of iron belonging
to them, a north and a fouth pole againſt
each piece of iron : then take two of the
four bars already made magnetical, and
place them together, ſo as to make a double bar in thickneſs, the north pole of one
even with the fouth pole of the other ; and
the remaining two being put to theſe in
ſuch a manner as to have two north and
two fouth poles together, ſeparate the north
from the fouth poles at one end, by a large
pin, and place them perpendicularly with
that end downward, on the middle of one
of the parallel bars, the two north poles
towards its fouth, and the two fouth poles
towards its north end ; ſlide them backward and forward, three or four times,
the whole length of the bar ; and re-
moving them from the middle of this,
place them on the middle of the other
bar, as before directed, and go over that
in the ſame manner : then turn both the
bars the other ſide upwards, and repeat the
former operation : this being done, take
the

the two from between the pieces of iron, and placing the outermoſt of the touching bars in their room, let the other two be the outermoſt of the four to touch theſe with : and this proceſs being repeated till each pair of bars have been touched three or four times over, which will give them a conſiderable magnetic power, put the half dozen together after the manner of the four, Fig. 3. and touch with them two pair of the hard bars, placed between their irons, at the diſtance of about half an inch from each other : then lay the ſoft bars aſide, and with the four hard ones let the other two be impregnated, Fig. 4. holding the touching bars apart, at the lower end, near two-tenths of an inch, to which diſtance let them be ſeparated, after they are ſet on the parallel bar, and brought together again before they are taken off.

This being obſerved, proceed according to the method deſcribed above, till each pair

pair has been touched two or three times over. But as this vertical way of touching a bar, will not give it quite fo much of the magnetic virtue as it will receive, let each pair be now touched once or twice over, in their parallel pofition between the irons, Fig. 5, with two of the bars held horizontally, or nearly fo; by drawing at the fame time the north of one from the middle over the fouth end, and the fouth of the other from the middle over the north end of a parallel bar; then bringing them to the middle again, without touching the parallel bar, give three or four of thefe horizontal ftrokes to each fide. The horizontal touch, after the vertical, will make the bars as ftrong as they can poffibly be made: as appears by their not receiving any additional ftrength, when the vertical touch is given by a greater number, and the horizontal, by bars of a fuperior magnetic power. This whole procefs may be gone through in about half an hour; and each

of

of the larger bars, if well hardened, may
be made to lift 28 troy ounces ; and sometimes more. And when thefe bars are
thus impregnated, they will give to an
hard bar of the fame fize, its full virtue
in lefs than two minutes ; and therefore
will anfwer all the purpofes of magnetifm
in navigation and experimental philofophy, much better than the loadftone,
which is well known not to have fufficient power to impregnate hard bars.
The half dozen being put into a cafe,
Fig. 6. in fuch manner, as that two poles
of the fame denomination may not be together, and their irons with them as one
bar, they will retain the virtue they have
received. But if their power fhould, by
making experiments, be ever fo far impaired, it may be reftored without any
foreign affiftance in a few minutes. And
if, out of curiofity, a much larger fet of
bars fhould be required, thefe will communicate to them a fufficient power to
proceed

proceed with, and they may in a fhort time, by the fame method, be brought to their full ftrength.

THE MAGNETIC PERSPECTIVE GLASS.

PROVIDE an ivory tube, about two inches and a half long, and of the form expreffed in Plate V. Fig. 2. The fides of this tube muft be thin enough to admit a confiderable quantity of light. It is to open at one end with a fcrew: at that end there muft be placed an eye-glafs A, of about two inches focus, and at the other end, any glafs you pleafe.

Have a fmall magnetic needle, Fig. 4. like that placed on a compafs. It muft be ftrongly touched, and fo placed at the bottom of the tube that it may turn freely round. It is to be fixed on the center of a fmall ivory circle C, of the thicknefs of a counter, which is placed on the object-glafs D, and painted black on the fide

6   next

next it. This circle muſt be kept faſt by a circular rim of paſteboard, that the needle may not riſe off its pivot, after the ſame manner as is in the compaſs. This tube will thus become a compaſs, ſufficiently tranſparent to ſhow the motions of the needle. The eye-glaſs ſerves more clearly to diſtinguiſh the direction of the needle; and the glaſs at the other end, merely to give the tube the appearance of a common perſpective.

It will appear by aphoriſm 8, that the needle in this tube, when placed over, and at a ſmall diſtance from, a magnet, or any machine in which it is contained, will neceſſarily place itſelf in a poſition directed by that magnet, and conſequently ſhow where the north and ſouth pole of it is placed. The north end of the needle conſtantly pointing to the ſouth end of the magnet.

This effect will take place, though the magnet be incloſed in a caſe of wood, or

VOL. III.   K   even

even metal, as the magnetic effluvia pene-
trates all bodies. You muſt obſerve, however, that the attracting magnet muſt not
be very far diſtant from the needle, eſpe-
cially if it be ſmall, as in that caſe its influence extends but to a ſhort diſtance.

This tube may be differently conſtructed by placing the needle in a perpendicular direction, on a ſmall axis of iron, on
which it muſt turn quite freely, between
two ſmall plates of braſs placed on each
ſide the tube : the two ends of the needle
ſhould be in exact equilibrium. The
north and ſouth ends of this needle will,
in like manner, be attracted by the ſouth
and north ends of the magnetic bar. The
former conſtruction, however, appears preferable, as it is more eaſily excited, and
the ſituation of the needle much more eaſily diſtinguiſhed.

THE

THE MAGNETIC WAND.

PROCURE a round ftick of ebony, or other wood, of about eight or ten inches long, and about half an inch thick. Let there be a hole bored through the length of it, of about two or three-tenths of an inch in diameter (fee Plate V. Fig. 5.) Provide a fmall fteel rod, and let it be very ftrongly impregnated by a good magnet. Place this rod in the hollow of the wand, and clofe it at each extremity, by two fmall ends of ivory A and B, that fcrew on, and are differently formed, that you may the more eafily remember the poles of the magnetic bar.

When you prefent the north pole of this wand to the fouth pole of a magnetic needle, fufpended freely on a pivot, or to a light body, fwimming on the furface of water, or any other fluid, and in which you have placed a magnetic bar, that body

K 2 will

will then approach the wand, and prefent that fide which contains the fouth end of the bar. On the contrary, if you prefent the north or fouth end of the wand to the north or fouth end of the needle, or of the bar, they will recede from it.

Obferve, that after the needle or the floating bar has retired from the wand, it will prefent the other pole to it ; therefore as foon as the needle retires, you muft withdraw the wand, or keep it conftantly prefented to the pole of the fame name. This wand is of ufe but in very few experiments. To give it more force it may be armed with iron, after the manner explained in the aphorifms.

RECREATION XXVIII.

The communicative crown.

TAKE a crown piece, and bore a hole in the side of it; in which place a piece of wire, or a large needle well polifhed, and ftrongly touched with a magnet. Then clofe the hole with a fmall piece of pewter, that it may not be perceived. Now the needle in the magnetic perfpective before defcribed, when it is brought near to this piece of money, will fix itfelf in a direction correfpondent to the wire or needle in that piece.

Defire any perfon to lend you a crown piece, which you dextroufly change for one that you have prepared as above. Then give the latter piece to another perfon, and leave him at liberty either to put it privately in a fnuff-box, or not; he is then to place the box on a table, and you are to tell him, by means of your glafs, if

K 3   the

the crown is or is not in the box. Then bringing your perfpective clofe to the box, you will know, by the motion of the needle, whether it be there or not ; for as the needle in the perfpective will always keep to the north of itfelf, if you don't perceive it has any motion, you conclude the crown is not in the box. It may happen, however, that the wire in the crown may be placed to the north, in which cafe you will be deceived. Therefore to be fure of fuccefs, when you find the needle in the perfpective remain ftationary, you may make fome pretence to defire the perfon to move the box into another pofition, by which you will certainly know if the crown piece be there or not.

You muft remember that the needle in the perfpective muft here be very fenfible, as the wire in the crown cannot poffibly have any great attractive force.

R E C R E-

RECREATION XXIX.

The magnetic table.

UNDER the top of a common table place a magnet that turns on a pivot, and fix a board under it, that nothing may appear. There may alfo be a drawer under the table, which you pull out to fhow that there is nothing concealed. At one end of the table there muft be a pin that communicates with the magnet, and by which it may be placed in different po- fitions : this pin muft be fo placed as not to be vifible by the fpectators. Strew fome fteel filings, or very fmall nails, over that part of the table where the mag- net is. Then afk any one to lend you a knife, or a key, which will then attract part of the nails or filings, in the fame manner as the iron attracts the needle, in the note to the twelfth aphorifm. Then placing your hand, in a carelefs manner,

K 4

on

on the pin at the end of the table, you alter the pofition of the magnet; and giving the key to any perfon you defire him to make the experiment, which he will then not be able to perform. You then give the key to another perfon, at the fame time placing the magnet, by means of the pin, in the firft pofition, when that perfon will immediately perform the experiment.

RECREATION XXX.

The myfterious watch.

YOU defire any perfon to lend you his watch, and afk him if he thinks it will or will not go, when it is laid on the table. If he fay it will, you place it over the end of the magnet, and it will prefently ftop *. You then mark with chalk, or a pencil, the precife point where you placed

* To perform this experiment you muft ufe a ftrong magnetic bar, and the balance of the watch muft not be of brafs, but fteel.

the

the watch, and moving the pofition of the magnet, as in the laft Recreation, you give the watch to another perfon, and defire him to make the experiment, in which he not fucceeding, you give it to a third perfon, at the fame time replacing the magnet, and he will immediately perform the experiment.

RECREATION   XXXI.

The bouquets.

IN a box of light wood, that fhuts with hinges, and is about nine or ten inches long, five or fix wide, and one inch thick, as ABCD (Pl. VII. Fig. 1.) fix a fmall vafe, that has a hole in one fide, through which is to pafs the end of a bouquet of artificial flowers; of which you are to have two, as F and G. The two principal ftalks of thefe bouquets are to be made of fteel, that has been ftrongly touched; and you are to obferve that the north pole of one of thefe bouquets is to be

placed

placed in the vafe, and the other is to be at the top of the flower. Both thefe wires, as well as well as all the others that compofe the flowers, are to be covered with filk.

You prefent one of thefe bouquets to any perfon, and give him the choice either of placing it privately in the vafe or not. Then, fhutting the box, he is to give it you. When applying the magnetic per-fpective to it, you difcover, by the mo-tion of the needle, whether it be there or not; for if it be not there, the needle will not fix itfelf to either end of the box.

You then prefent both the flowers, and give him the choice of placing either of them, in like manner, in the box; and by applying the perfpective as before, you difcover, by the fixing of the needle, which of the bouquets is there placed. You may yet farther diverfify this Recre-ation by having three flowers, of which one

one muft not be impregnated; and give the perfon the choice of placing either of them in the box : but in this cafe he muft put in one of them.

You muft obferve that the needle in the perfpective, in making this experiment, muft be very fenfible : it will be proper to try its force on the ftalk of the bouquet before the flowers are placed on it.

RECREATION XXXII.

The magnetic dial.

PROVIDE a circle of wood or ivory, of about five or fix inches diameter, as Pl. VII. Fig. 2. which muft turn quite free on the ftand B, in the circular border A : on the circle muft be placed the dial of pafteboard C, whofe circumference is to be divided into twelve equal parts, in which muft be infcribed the numbers from one to twelve, as on a common dial. There muft be a fmall

groove

groove in the circular frame D, to receive the pasteboard circle : and observe that the dial must be made to turn so free, that it may go round, without moving the circular border in which it is placed.

Between the pasteboard circle and the bottom of the frame, place a small artificial magnet E, Fig. 3. that has a hole in its middle, or a small protuberance.   On the outside of the frame place a small pin P, which serves to show where the magnetic needle I, that is placed on a pivot at the center of the dial, is to stop.   This needle must turn quite free on its pivot, and its two sides should be in exact equilibrium.

Then provide a small bag, that has five or six divisions, like a lady's work bag, but smaller. In one of these divisions put small square pieces of pasteboard, on which are wrote the numbers from one to twelve; and if you please you may put several of each number.   In each of the other

other divifions you muft put twelve or
more like pieces, obferving that all the
pieces in each divifion muft be marked
with the fame number.

Now the needle being placed upon its
pivot, and turned quickly about, it will
neceffarily ftop at that point where the
north end of the magnetic bar is placed :
and which you previoufly know by the
fituation of the fmall pin in the circular
border.

You therefore prefent to any perfon
that divifion of the bag which contains
the feveral pieces on which is wrote the
number oppofite to the north end of the
bar, and tell him to draw any one of them
he pleafes. Then placing the needle on
the pivot, you turn it quickly about, and
it will neceffarily ftop, as we have already
faid, at that particular number.

Another Recreation may be made with
the fame dial, by defiring two perfons to
draw

draw, each of them, one number out of two
different divifions of the bag, and if their
numbers, when added together, exceed
twelve, the needle or index will ftop at the
number they exceed it : but if they do not
amount to twelve, the index will ftop at the
fum of thofe two numbers. In order to perform this Recreation you muft place the
pin againft the number five, if the two
numbers to be drawn from the bag be ten
and feven : or againft nine, if they be feven
and two.

If this Recreation be made immediately
after the former, as it eafily may, by dextroufly moving the pin, it will appear ftill
the more extraordinary.

R E C R E-

RECREATION XXXIII.

The magnetical cards.

ON the pasteboard circle mentioned in the preceding Recreation, instead of the twelve numbers, inscribe the four suits of the cards, and the eight cards of each suit that are used at piquet, in the following order :

Divisions.

1. Ace
2. King
3. Knave
4. A heart
5. Queen
6. A diamond
7. An eight
8. A spade
9. A ten
10. A seven
11. A club
12 A nine,

as is expressed in Plate VII. Fig. 4. You must have two similar needles, which

8   how—

however muſt be diſtinguiſhable by ſome
private mark. Theſe needles muſt have
their oppoſite points touched. Of the eight
cards of piquet inſcribed on the circle
there are only four that are of uſe here,
which are thoſe that are oppoſite the four
pips: the others however are uſed in the
ſecond part of this Recreation.

When you place that needle or index
on the pivot whoſe pointed end is touched, it will ſtop at one of the four pips
againſt which you have placed the pin in
the frame: then taking that needle off,
and placing the other, it will ſtop at the
oppoſite point.

Therefore deſire a perſon to draw a
card from a piquet pack, offering that
card againſt which you have placed the
pin of the dial, which you may eaſily do
by having a long card, as is explained in the
firſt volume. Tell the perſon who draws
the

the card to keep it clofe, that it may not be feen. Then give him one of the two needles, and defire him to place it on the pivot and turn it about, when he will fee it ftop at the colour of the card he has chofe: then taking that needle off, change it dextroufly for the other, and give that to another perfon, telling him to place and turn it in like manner, and it will ftop at the name of the card the firft perfon chofe.

If the firft perfon fhould not draw the card you intend, you cannot directly perform this Recreation: therefore to prevent any fufpicion that you have failed in your defign, cut the cards yourfelf at the large card, and let him put the card he drew under that card, then give them to one or more perfons to cut, and when you perceive the long card is at bottom, you tell the perfon that the card he drew is at the top of the pack: and after this little

VOL. III. L diverfion

diverfion you may begin the Recreation again.

The foregoing Recreation may be diverfified by having a pack of piquet cards in which there are two longer than the reft, and that anfwer to two that are oppofite each other on the circle, and were not ufed in the other Recreation. Then let two perfons draw each of them one of thofe two cards.

Prefent the needle that will point to the fecond perfon's card to the firft perfon: after which take it off, and changing it privately, prefent to the fecond perfon the needle that will point to the firft perfon's card. You will obferve that this Recreation does not fhow the particular fuite in which the two cards were drawn.

RECRE-

RECREATION XXXIV.

The dextrous painter.

PROVIDE two fmall boxes as M and
N, (Pl. VIII. Fig. 1.) four inches wide,
and four inches and a half long.   Let the
box M be half an inch deep, and N two-
thirds of an inch.   They muft both open
with hinges and fhut with a clafp.   Have
four fmall pieces of light wood, as OPQR
in the fame plate, of the fame fize with
the infide of the box M, and about one
third of an inch thick.   In each of thefe
let there be a groove, as A B, E F, C D,
G H, thefe grooves muft be in the middle,
and parallel to two of the fides.   In each
of thefe grooves place a ftrong artificial
magnet, as V.   The poles of thefe magnets muft be properly difpofed with regard
to the figures that are to be painted on
the boards; as is expreffed in the plate.
Cover the bars with paper to prevent their
being feen;   but take care in pafting it on

L 2   not

not to wet the bars, as they will thereby
ruſt, which will conſiderably impair their
virtue. When you have painted ſuch ſubjeЄts as you chooſe, you may cover them
with a very thin clear glaſs.

At the center of the box N, place a pivot T, on which a ſmall circle of paſteboard O P Q R, Fig. 2. is to turn quite
free; under which is to be a touched
needle S. Divide this circle into four
parts, which are to be diſpoſed with re-
gard to the poles of the needle, as is expreſſed in the figure. In theſe four diviſions you are to paint the ſame ſubjeЄts as
are on the four boards, but reduced to a
ſmaller compaſs. Cover the inſide of the
top of this box with a paper M, (ſee Fig.
1.) in which muſt be an opening D, at
about half an inch from the center of the
box, that you may perceive, ſucceſſively,
the four ſmall piЄtures on the paſteboard
circle juſt mentioned. This opening is
to ſerve as the cloth on which the little
                                        painter

7

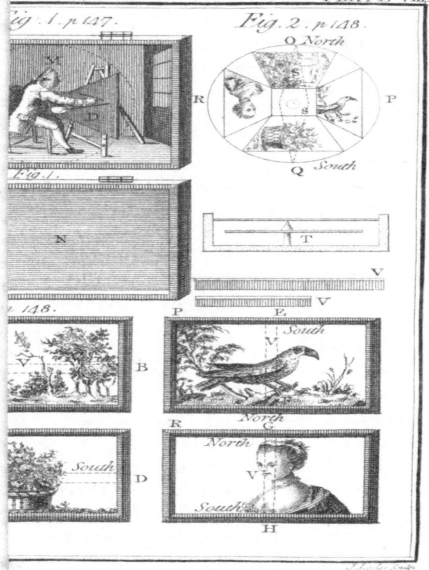

Fig. 1. p 147.

Fig. 2. p 148.

O North

S

s

P

Q South

Fig. 1.

N

T

V

V

P

E

South

M

North

G

R

North

V

South

H

B

D

J. Lodge Sculp

painter is fuppofed to draw one of the pictures. You may cover the top of the box, if you pleafe, with a thin glafs.

Then give the firft box to any perfon, and tell him to place any one of the four pictures in it privately, and when he has clofed it, to give it you. You then place the other box over it, when the moveable circle, with the needle, will turn till it comes in the fame pofition with the bar in the firft box. It will then appear that the little dexterous painter has already copied the picture that is inclofed in the firft box.

RECREATION XXXV.

The cylindric oracle.

PROVIDE a hollow cylinder of about
fix inches high, and three wide, as
AB, Pl. IX. Fig. 1. Its cover CD, muſt
be made to fix on any way. On one fide of
this box or cylinder let there be a groove,
nearly of the fame length with that
fide; in which place a fmall ſteel bar as H,
that is ſtrongly impregnated; with the
north pole next the bottom of the cylinder.
On the upper fide of the cover defcribe a
circle, and divide it into ten equal parts,
in which are to be wrote the numbers
from one to ten, as is expreſſed in the
figure.   Place a pivot at the center of this
circle, and have ready a magnetic needle.
You are then to provide a bag, in which
there are feveral divifions, like that defcribed in the 32d Recreation.   In each
of thefe divifions put a number of papers,
                                        on

on which the fame, or fimilar queftions, are wrote.

In the cylinder put feveral different an- fwers to each queftion, and feal them up in the manner of fmall letters. On each of thefe letters or anfwers is to be wrote one of the numbers on the dial or circle at the top of the box. You are fuppofed to know the number of the anfwers to each queftion.

You then offer one of the divifions of the bag, obferving which divifion it is, to any perfon, and defire him to draw one of the papers. Next put the top on the cylinder, with that number which is wrote on the anfwer directly over the bar. Then placing the needle on the pivot you turn it brifkly about, and it will naturally ftop at the number over the bar. You then defire the perfon who drew the quef- tion to obferve the number at which the needle ftands, and to fearch in the box

L 4

for

for a paper with the fame number, which he will find to contain the anfwer.

You may repeat the experiment by offering another divifion of the bag to the fame or another perfon: and placing the number that correfponds to the anfwer over the magnetic bar, proceed as before.

It is eafy to conceive of feveral anfwers to the fame queftion. For example, fuppofe the queftion to be. Is it proper to marry ?

Anfwer 1. While you are young not yet, when you are old not at all.

2. Marry in hafte, and repent at leifure.

3. Yes, if you can get a good fortune, for fomething has fome favour, but nothing has no flavour.

4. No, if you are apt to be out of humour with yourfelf; for then you will have two perfons to quarrel with.

5. Yes,

5. Yes, if you are fure to get a good hufband (wife); for that is the greateft bleffing of life. But take care you are fure.

6. No, if the perfon you would marry is an angel; unlefs you will be content to live with a devil.

RECREATION XXXVI.

The myftical dial.

IN a box A B C D, (Plate IX. Fig. 2.) of about four inches fquare, and that fhuts with a hinge, let there be an opening O, of three inches and a half fquare, and half an inch deep.

Provide four fquare pieces of wood E, F, G, H, Fig. 3. of the fame fize with the opening in the box. On thefe pieces defcribe the cirles I L M N, which divide into four equal parts by the diagonals I M and L N and then fubdivide the parts NM and IL into four other equal parts: in each fquare

piece

piece make a groove, as P, Q, R, S, and in each groove place a magnetic bar: then cover the fquares with paper, and write on them the words two, fix, eight, and twelve, as is exprefled in the figure.

On another fquare piece, Fig. 4. of the fame fize with the furface of the box, defcribe a circle, and divide it into four equal parts by the diagonals M P and N O: then fubdivide each of thofe four parts into four other equal parts; forming in the whole fixteen equal divifions, in which you are to write the numbers exprefled in that figure. You will obferve that on the fide M N, are wrote the numbers that are in the other four fquares; on the oppofite fide O P, the double of thofe numbers; on the fide N P, the half of thofe numbers; and on the oppofite fide M O, the triple of the firft numbers. Fix a pivot at the center of this circle, and on it place a magnetic needle.

You

You then give the four square pieces to a person, and desire him to put any one of them in the box, then to shut it, and place it himself on the table. He is next to choose whether the index of the dial shall point to the number of the square he has placed in the box, its half, its double, or triple; and you then place the dial over the box in the proper position. For the north pole of all the bars in the four square pieces being on the same side, the index will necessarily stop at that side; and consequently, as the dial is placed, will point to the whole, the half, the double, or triple of each number.

R E C R E A T I O N XXXVII.

The enchanted ewer.

FIX a common ewer as A, Plate X. Fig. 1. of about twelve inches high, upon a square stand B C, in one side of which there must be a drawer D, of about four inches square and half an inch deep. In the ewer place a hollow tin cone, inverted, as A B, Fig. 2. of about four inches and a half diameter at top, and two inches at bottom ; and at the bottom of the ewer there must likewise be a hole of two inches diameter.

Upon the stand, at about an inch distance from the bottom of the ewer, place a small convex mirror H, Fig. 2. of such convexity that a person's visage, when viewed in it, at about fifteen inches distance, may not appear above two inches and a half long.

Upon

3

9

8

Upon the stand likewife, at the point I, Fig. 2. place a pivot of half an inch high, on which muft be fixed a touched needle R Q, inclofed in a circle of very thin pafteboard O S, Fig. 3. of five inches diameter. Divide this pafteboard into four parts, in each of which draw a fmall circle: and in three of thefe circles paint a head as *x*, *y*, *z*, the drefs of each of which is to be different, one, for example, having a turban, another a hat, and the other a woman's cap. Let that part which contains the face in each picture be cut out: and let the fourth circle be entirely cut out; as it is expreffed in the figure. You muft obferve that the poles of the needle are to be difpofed in the fame manner as in the plate.

You are next to provide four fmall frames of wood or pafteboard, *w*, *x*, *y*, *z*, Fig. 4. each of the fame fize with the infide of the drawer. On thefe frames muft be painted the fame figures as on the circular

cular pasteboard, with this difference, that there must be no part of them cut out. Behind each of these pictures place a magnetic bar, in the same direction as is expressed in the plate; and cover them over with paper, that they may not be visible.

Matters being thus prepared, you first place in the drawer the frame *w*, on which there is nothing painted. You then pour a small quantity of water into the ewer, and desire the company to look into it, asking them if they see their own figures as they are. Then you take out the frame *w*, and give the three others to any one, desiring him to choose in which of those dresses he would appear. Then put the frame with the dress he has chose in the drawer, and a moment after, the person looking into the ewer will see his own face surrounded with the dress of that picture.

This recreation, well performed, is highly agreeable. As the pasteboard circle

B

cle can contain only three heads, you may have feveral fuch circles, but you muft then have feveral other frames: and the ewer muft be made to take off from the ftand.

RECREATION XXXVIII.

The magician's circles.

LET there be two boxes A and B, Pl. X. Fig. 5. of about fix inches fquare, and connected by the piece C, of one inch and a half wide. The depth of the boxes muft be one inch, and that of the piece half an inch. In thefe boxes and the piece place the movement A B, Fig. 6. compofed of two horizontal wheels D and E, that have the fame number of teeth, and two pinions F and G. The axis of the wheel D muft pafs through the top of the box; and on it muft be placed a hand, by which it may be turned about; but that of E muft end beneath the cover of the box; a magnetic bar being placed on it, and above the box, on a fmall pivot, muft be placed a touched needle. This

move-

movement fhould be fo contrived as not to make any noife by its motion.

Draw a magic fquare in the following manner, confifting of twenty-five leffer fquares, numbered; and each line of which, whether read horizontally or perpendicularly, contains five words that give an anfwer to a queftion propofed. Let the five queftions be as follows:

	1.	2.	3.	4.	5.
1.	Are	you	pleafed	with	matrimony?
2.	What	does	all	times	pleafe?
3.	Should	we	wifh	for	inheritance?
4.	Do	you	defire	more	riches?
5.	What	pleafure	is	moft	defireable?

Then draw the fquare thus.

Magic Square.

1. I love	2. quite	3. well	4. my	5. hufband
6. quite	7. pleafes	8. what	9. wealth	10. brings
11. well	12. what	13. man	14. craves	15. delight
16. my	17 wealth	18. craves	19. much	20. encreafing
21. hufband	22. brings	23. delights	24. encreafing	25. ever

On

On each fide of the boxes place a fquare pafteboard of the fame dimenfion, and on that of A draw a circle, and divide it into thirty equal parts On that of B, draw likewife a circle, and divide it into fifteen equal parts. In the divifions of the circle A, write the words contained in the firft five columns of the following table, which compofe the foregoing queftions in the order they are there numbered. That is, the word *are* in the firft divifion, the word *be* in the fecond divifion, the word *you* in the third, the word *what* in the fourth divifion, &c. On the fifteen divifions of the circle B, write the words in the order they ftand in the laft column of this table. In the firft circle the words muft be wrote from right to left, and in the other from left to right.

Order of placing the words of the questions and answers on the two circles.

No.	1 question	2 question	3 question	4 question	5 question	No.	Answers
1	1 are / or / 2 be					1	I love
2	3 you					2	quite
3	5 content	4 what	6 should			3	well
4	7 with			8 do	10 what	4	my
5	9 matrimony					5	husband
6		10 does / or / 12 can	14 we	16 you	18 pleasure	6	pleases
7		13 all				7	what
8		15 times				8	wealth
9		17 please	19 wish / or / 20 pray			9	brings
10			21 for	22 desire		10	man
11			23 inheritance	25 more / or / 26 greater	24 is	11	craves
12				27 riches		12	delights
13					28 most	13	much
14					29 desireable / or	14	encreasing
15					30 estimable	15	ever

The words being thus tranfcribed on the dials, the hands of both of them are to be placed to the correfponding divifions ; for example, when the index of the dial A, is placed to the word *are*, that of the dial B, muft direct to the divifion which contains *I love* ; and fo of the reft. You muft then write on five cards the five fore-going queftions, that is, one of them on each card.

Matters being thus prepared, you prefent the five cards to any perfon, and defire him to choofe one of them, and then let him direct the index of the firft dial fuccefively to each of the five words which compofe that queftion : while another perfon, placed by the dial to which the touched needle is placed, writes down the words it fuccefively points to, and they will be found to form the anfwer. The moft remarkable circumftance in this recreation is, that the fifteen words on the dial B, give proper anfwers to the five

M 2

queftions

questions on the other dial, which contain thirty words; and that every answer consists of the same number of words with the question.

These dials, by means of pullies, may communicate when placed on the opposite sides of a room: and this experiment may be diversified, by having several dials to place over the movement, with various words or figures: the foregoing serving only as a specimen of the manner of performing recreations of this sort.

RECREATION XXXIX.

The box and dice.

MAKE a hollow pedestal as CA, (Pl. XI. Fig. 1.) twelve inches long, nine wide, and one deep. The cover of this pedestal must be made to slide on and off, and not be above two-tenths of an inch thick. Toward the part A of the cover describe the circle B, which is to be

divided

divided into twenty equal parts; and on these parts mark the different points that can be thrown by two dice *. At the center place a pivot, on which a magnetic needle is to turn.

On the bottom of the inside of this pedestal, and directly under the circle at top, describe another circle M, which must be divided and marked in the same manner. At the center fix a magnetic bar by a screw, so that it may be easily placed in any position; but not move of itself.

You must have two needles, the point of one being north and the other south: they should be in appearance quite similar; but there must be, however, some mark by which you can distinguish them.

* The number of different points that can be thrown by two dice is twenty-one, of which there are only twenty here, as the divisions are obliged to be diametrically opposite each other: that number however is quite sufficient for the present purpose.

M 3 On

On the pedeftal place a vafe D E, of tin
or pafteboard, about twelve inches high.
In the fide of the vafe there muft be two
parts that open, one at F G, and the other
at G H. Thefe openings fhould not be
deeper than the depth of one die, nor
wider than two; and they muft be made
to fhut quite clofe, that the places where
they open may not appear. The cover of
the vafe D, muft take off. There muft be
a communication between the top and the
divifion G H, and in that divifion are to
to be placed two dice of any number. In
the part I K muft be placed the flider S T;
which is exactly of the fame length, and
open next S, where muft be placed two
dice that contain the points at which one
of the needles is to ftop : and in the divifion F G, two other dice that are to contain the points at which the other needle
is to ftop. The bar within the pedeftal is
fuppofed to be previoufly fixed to the
points that anfwer to the dice.

Matters

2

Matters being thus prepared, you open
the part G H, and taking out those dice,
you throw them in at the top, and show
that they will fall into the same place
again.   You take them out a second time
and give them to any person, telling him
to throw them in at top.   In the mean
time you incline the vase toward your left
hand, when the slider at I K will come to
G H, and thereby prevent the dice that
are thrown in at top from falling into that
division, by stopping up the passage. You
then present him with the proper needle,
which he places on the pivot and turns
briskly about, and when it stops you tell
him that that the dice in the vase will
have the same points with that division at
which it has stopped.   Which on your
opening the upper division he will find to
be true.   You then take those dice out,
and give them to another person : and taking the needle off the pivot dextrously,
change it for the other.   You desire that
person to throw the dice in at top, and

give

give him the proper needle: and when it stops, you open the division F G, and taking out thofe dice, he will find them alfo anfwer to the points on the division of the circle where the needle ftopped.

RECREATION   XL.

The box of flowers.

PROVIDE a box of light wood, eight inches long, five wide, and one inch and a half deep, (Pl. XI. Fig. 2.) provide alfo two cafes F 3 and F 4, five inches long, four wide, and an inch and a half thick. Thefe muft be made hollow on each fide in the manner as is expreffed in the profile E. In each of them there muft be a groove, that contains a bar O, ftrongly impregnated; the poles of thefe bars are to be difpofed in the manner expreffed in the figure: toward the part G, there muft be a flider that holds a glafs, and the fides of the cafes muft be clofed.

In

In each of the four hollow parts in thefe two cafes, and under the glaffes, place four fmall natural flowers, of different forts, and let them be in oppofite direc-tions, that is, the top of one flower to be level with the bottom of that on the other fide.

In whatever pofition thefe cafes are placed in the box, the poles of the bars next the hinges, will have a determinate direction.   If the north pole of the bar at-tract the needle in the magnetic perfpective at the point X, it is the rofe that is there placed.   If the fouth attract the needle, it is the jonquil.   It will be the fame when thofe two poles attract the needle at Z.

If the fouth pole attract the needle at the point Y, it is the carnation that is there placed.   If the north pole attract it there, it is the hyacinth : and it will be the fame when thofe two poles attract the needle at &.   You muft remember that
the

the north pole of the bar attracts the south
of the needle, and the south the north.
You therefore give the two cases, containing the flowers, to any one, and let him
place them, in what position he please, in
the box: and then, by the aid of the magnetic perspective. you tell him immediately where each flower is placed.

RECREATION XLI.

The box of metals.

PROVIDE a wooden box about thir-
teen inches long and seven wide, as A
B C D, (Pl. XII. Fig. 1.)   The cover of
this box should be as thin as possible.

Have six small boxes or tablets, about
an inch deep; all of the same size and
form, as E F G H I K, that they may in-
discriminately go into similar holes made
in the bottom of the large box.

In each of these tablets is to be placed a
small magnetic bar, and their poles are to
be

be difposed as is expreffed in the figure.
Cover each of thefe tablets with a thin
plate of one of the fix following metals;
viz. gold, filver, copper, iron, pewter, and
lead. You muft alfo have a magnetic perfpective, at the end of which is to be two
circles, one divided into fix equal parts,
and the other into four, as in Fig. 2. from
the center of which there muft be drawn
an index N, whofe point is to be placed to
the north.

Therefore, when you are on the fide
C D of the box, and hold your perfpective
over any one of the tablets that are placed
on the holes E, F, G, fo that the index
drawn on the circle is perpendicular to the
fide A B, the needle in the perfpective
will have its fouth pole directed to the
letter that denotes the metal contained in
that tablet. When you hold the perfpective over one of the boxes placed in the
holes H, I, K, fo that the index drawn
on the circle is perpendicular to the fide
C D,

C D, the fouth pole of the needle will in like manner exprefs the name of the metal inclofed.

If the under-fide of any one of the tablets be turned upward, the needle will be flower in its motion, on account of the greater diftance of the bar. The gold and filver will ftill have the fame direction, but the four other metals will be expreffed by the letters on the interior circle.

If any one of the metals be taken away, the needle will not then take any of the above directions, but naturally point to the north; and its motion will be much flower.

You therefore give the box to any one, and leave him at liberty to difpofe all the tablets in what manner, and with which fide upward he pleafe, and even to take any one of them away. Then by the aid of your perfpective you tell him immediately the name of the metal on each tablet, and of that he has taken away.

This

This box of metals * will, on comparifon, be found far to exceed that which has been publicly exhibited: for that being compofed of fix tablets, of which two only differ in form, admits but of fix different difpofitions, whereas in this the tablets may be placed 720 different ways. In the other you muft alfo know the particular fide of the box, which in this is not at all neceffary, Nay, you may here diftinguifh each metal, though the box be completely covered with paper; for the effect of the needle will be always the fame. The recreations with this box are therefore much more extraordinary, and its conftruction at the fame time more fimple.

* It was invented by the Duke de Pequigny, and by him communicated to M. Guyot.

RECREATION   XLII.

The magnetic oracle.

IN a box a foot long, three inches and three quarters wide, and one inch deep, make three equal divisions, A, B, C, (Plate XII. Fig. 3.) Have eight small boxes or tablets of the same size with the division B of the box, into which they should go only one-fourth of an inch deep. In two of these tablets make a groove from the opposite angles, going from right to left, in which place the bars A, B, Fig. 4. and in two others a groove that goes in like manner from left to right, in which put the bars C, D. In two others a groove that divides them vertically into two equal parts, and place in them the bars E, F: and in the two last a groove that divides them horizontally, in which place the bars G, H. The poles of each of these bars are to be placed in the manner expressed in the figure.

Upon

Upon a board five inches fquare defcribe the circle N O, (Fig. 5.) which is to
be divided into eight equal parts, in each
of which write one of the numbers 1, 2,
3, 4, 5, 6, 7, 8, as in the figure, and let
this board be placed on the part B of the
box A B C.

Provide 32 fmall rundlets of wood or
ivory, of three quarters of an inch long,
and pierced with a hole of about one quarter of an inch diameter, Fig. 3. and mark
thefe barrels with the numbers 1, 2, 3,
4, 5, 6, 7, 8.

Then cover the tablets with paper to
conceal the magnetic bars ; and on each of
them write fome queftion, in fuch manner that the laft word may direct to the
north pole of the bar.

On fmall flips of paper write four different anfwers to each queftion, then roll
them up and put them into the little
rund-

rundlets. You muſt obſerve that the ſame number is to be wrote on four of the rundlets, and one of the four anſwers put into each of them ; according to the direction of the needle of the dial. The little barrels being thus prepared, are to be placed on the two ſides A and C of the box, Fig. 3.

You then give the eight tablets to any one, and leave him at liberty to place which of them he pleaſe on the box ; which being done he is to turn the rundlet round, and when it ſtops he is to chooſe one of thoſe rundlets that are marked with the number where it ſtops, in which he will neceſſarily find the proper anſwer. To diverſify this Recreation, the favourable anſwers may be placed on one ſide of the box, and the unfavourable on the other, ſo that you may tell him to chooſe either the one or the other.

RECRE-

PLATE XII.

p.171.

C

North

North

North

B

D

J. Lodge Sculp

RECREATION XLIII.

The incomprehensible card.

INSERT in the middle of a card, and parallel to its two longest sides, part of a watch spring, as thin as possible, and strongly impregnated: let it be so concealed as not to afford the least suspicion. This card should be a little longer than the others of the pack in which it is placed.

Offer any one to draw a card out of the pack, and present the long card dextrously to his hand. You then give him all the cards, and leave him at liberty to replace that card in the pack or not. He is then to lay the pack on the table, and by applying your magnetic perspective, you will discover whether the card be there or not.

If the perſon ſhould not draw that card, you muſt be ready with ſome other recreation, to prevent ſuſpicion of having failed in your deſign.

RECREATION XLIV.

The two magical cards.

PROVIDE a box A B C D (Plate XII. Fig. 6.) four inches ſquare and three quarters of an inch deep. Cover its top with a paſteboard, in which there is an opening at A. At the center of this box let there be a pivot that ſupports a circle of paſteboard E F, on which is painted two cards : and at its center is to be a magnetic needle ; as is expreſſed in the figure.

Now if you lay the magnetic wand, deſcribed at the beginning of this volume, ſo that the north pole of the bar it contains be next the middle of one of the ſides of the box, the magnetic needle, with the
paſte-

pasteboard circle, will turn so that its south pole will be next the wand. But if the south end of the wand be next the box, the north end of the needle will present itself, and consequently one or the other of the cards will be visible. You must therefore have a pack of cards in which one of the same sort with those painted on the circle is a small matter longer, and the other, wider than the rest.

Being thus prepared, you desire two persons to draw each one card, taking care to present those two cards, so artfully that they can scarce draw any other. Then holding the wand carelesly in your hand, you ask one of the parties whether his own or the other person's card shall appear first. You then touch the box with your magic wand, and lay it on the table, as if the more easily to open the box. After giving the needle a short time to settle, you open the box and shew the card desired.

N 2 To

To fhow the other card, you place the box on the table with the other fide next the wand.

You may fhuffle the cards before you offer them, as you will always diftinguifh by the touch where the two cards are. If the parties fhould not draw thofe two cards, you muft be ready with fome other amufement, that it may not be perceived you have failed.

RECREATION XLV.

The magnetic planetarium.

CONSTRUCT a round box I L M N, of eight or nine inches diameter, and half an inch deep, (Plate XIII. Fig. 1.) On its bottom fix a circle of pafteboard, on which draw the central circle A, and the feven circumjacent circles B, C, D, E, F, G, H. Divide the central circle into feven equal parts by the lines A B, A C, A D, A E, A F, A G, and A H, which

muft

muft pafs through the centers of the other circles and divide each of them into two equal parts. Then divide the circumference of each of thofe circles into 14 equal parts, as in the figure.

You are likewife to have another pafteboard of the fame figure, and divided in the fame manner, which muft turn freely in the box, by means of an axis placed on a pivot, one end of which is to be fixed in the center of the circle A. See Fig. 2.

On each of the feven fmaller circles at the bottom of the box, place a magnetic bar, two inches long, in the fame direction with the diameters of thofe circles, and their poles in the fituations expreffed in the figure.

There muft be an index O, like that of the hour-hand of a dial, which is to be fixed on the axis of the central circle, and by which the pafteboard circle in the box

N 3   may

may be turned about. There muſt be alſo a needle P, that will turn freely on the axis, without moving the circular paſteboard.

In each of the ſeven diviſions of the central circle write a different queſtion, and in another circle, divided into 12 parts, you may write the names of the 12 months. In each of the ſeven circles write two anſwers to each queſtion, obſerving that there muſt be but ſeven words in each anſwer; in the following manner.

In the firſt diviſion of the circle G, which is oppoſite the firſt queſtion, write the firſt word of the firſt anſwer. In the ſecond diviſion of the next circle write the ſecond word; and ſo on to the laſt word, which will be in the ſeventh diviſion of the ſeventh circle.

In the eighth diviſion of the firſt circle write the firſt word of the ſecond anſwer:

in

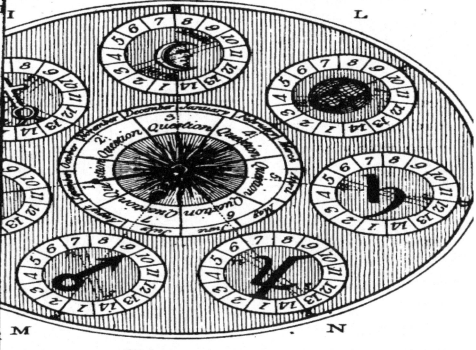

PLATE X

Fig. 1. p. 180.

Fig. 2. p. 181.

J. Lodge.

in the ninth divifion of the fecond circle write the fecond word of the fame anfwer; and fo on to the fourteenth divifion of the feventh circle, which muft contain the laft word of that anfwer.

The fame muft be done for all the feven queftions, and to each of them muft be affigned two anfwers, the words of which are to be difperfed through the feven circles.

At the center of each of thefe circles place a pivot, and have two magnetic needles, the pointed end of one of which muft be north, and the other fouth.

Now, the index of the central circle being directed to any one of the queftions, if you place one of the two magnetic needles on each of the feven leffer circles, they will fix themfelves according to the direction of the bars on the correfpondent

N 4 circles,

circles, at the bottom of the box, and confequently point to the feven words that compofe the anfwer. If you place one of the other needles on each circle, it will point to the words that are diametrically oppofite to thofe of the firft anfwer, the north pole being in the place of the fouth pole of the other.

You therefore prefent this planetarium to any perfon, and defire him to choofe one of the queftions there wrote; and you then fet the index of the central circle to that queftion, and putting one of the needles on each of the feven circles, you turn it about, and when they all fettle they will point to the feven words that compofe the anfwer. The two anfwers may be one favourable and the other unfavourable: and the different needles will ferve to diverfify the anfwers when you repeat the experiment.

There

There may alfo be a moveable needle to place againft the names of the months ; and when the party has fixed upon a queftion, you place that needle againft the month in which he was born, which will give the bufinefs an air of more myftery.

At the center of the large circle may be the figure of the fun, and on each of the feven fmaller circles one of the characters of the five planets, together with the earth and moon. This Recreation, well executed, is one of the moft entertaining that magnetifm has produced.

CON-

CONSTRUCTION OF THE MAGNETI-
CAL AND MECHANICAL TABLE.

LET the table A B C D (Plate XIV,
Fig. 1, and 2.) be conſtructed by an
able workman, as near as poſſible after
the following plan and dimenſions.

Firſt, this table muſt be five feet long,
by two feet and a half wide. Its top muſt
be only half an inch thick, except at the
edge, which is to be one inch and a half
thick, and go out beyond the feet of the
table about an inch. This precaution is
quite neceſſary, that the magnetic apparatus concealed beneath the ſurface of the
table may be the nearer to the pieces
placed on it ; and that there may be no
room to imagine that there are any parts
concealed.

Secondly, the four feet E, F, G, H,
Fig. 2. as well as the two croſs-pieces
L, L, muſt be hollow, being formed of
four

four pieces of wood half an inch thick, and two inches wide, and confequently the fpace between them a fquare inch.

In the third place, there muft be a fecond furface to the table, placed under the other, and at one inch and a half diftance from it. Fourthly, at one end of the table-frame, and parallel with the crofs-pieces L, L, there muft be a ftep M N, which joins to the frame; the joints of this ftep are likewife to be hollow, and communicate with the two hind feet of the table. This table muft be made with great care, that there may be no room to fufpect there are any cavities in the legs or top: and if any of the joinings fhould appear, they muft be painted to prevent all fufpicion. The table being thus prepared may be covered with a green cloth, on which are to be placed the different pieces hereafter defcribed, by which the fubfequent recreations are to be performed.

On

On the fide of the lower plane of the table next A B, at eight inches diftance from the point O, and at the point P, fix the piece Q R, Fig. 3. compofed of a pulley S, of fix inches diameter, and one-third of an inch thick, on which is fixed a brafs rod ; to one end of which muft be faftened two magnetic bars, eight inches long, and bound together by four brafs rings ; or a fingle bar, ftrongly impregnated ; or elfe an impregnated horfe-fhoe, placed as X Y Z.

Beneath this pulley, and at its center, fix the brafs barrel X, of one inch and a half diameter, and half an inch thick, in which fix the fpring of a clock. At the end of the axis of the pulley, and beyond the brafs barrel, let there be a fquare hole, that is to come out, under the table, and clofe to it, and by which is to be faftened a fmall wheel with a catch, that the fpring in the barrel may be contracted or extended at pleafure.   Round the pulley let there

go

Letters	Cards		Numbers
A	Ace		1
B	King		2
C	Queen		
	Knave		
D	Ten	Hearts	3
E	Nine		4
F	Eight		
	Seven		
G	Ace		5
H	King		6
I	Queen		
	Knave		7
J	Ten	Spades	
K	Nine		8
L	Eight		9
	Seven		
M	Ace		10
N	King		
O	Queen		11
	Knave		
P	Ten	Diamonds	12
Q	Nine		
R	Eight		13
S	Seven		14
T	Ace		15
U	King		
W	Queen		¾
	Knave	Clubs	
X	Ten		½
Y	Nine		
	Eight		¾
Z	Seven		

V　　C　　O

D

F　　　　E

go a fmall ftring, fuch as is not much apt to dilate or contract *. It fhould firft pafs over a fmall pulley near the opening into the foot H, and then over another at the bottom of the fame foot †, and oppofite to the communication with the ftep, that it may go out behind the partition W.

Againft the other fide of the partition there is to be placed a table (Plate XV.) of two feet and a half long, and placed at a convenient height for the perfon who is to draw the ftring that communicates with the magnetic apparatus, clearly to diftin-guifh the numbers, letters, and words, there wrote.

The table is thus formed. Firft, meafure the exact diftance that the cord paffes over while the pulley makes a com—

* It may be braided like a lace, as that is not much fubject to contract.
† Thefe pullies fhould be fixed on their axes, that they may not make any noife in turning.

plete revolution, and mark that diftance on the table, as from V to Z.

Have three circles of wood, covered with paper, as A, B, and C, Fig. 1, 4, and 5. Divide that of A into 24 equal parts, and in each of thofe parts write one of the 24 letters of the alphabet. Divide the firft column of the table into the fame number of equal parts, and in each of them write the fame letters and in the fame order.

Then divide the circle B into 32 equal parts, in each of which write the name of one of the cards of piquet. Divide the fecond column of the table in the fame number of equal parts, and in them write the fame names in the fame order.

Laftly, divide the circle C, into 18 equal parts, in each of which write one of the numbers from 1 to 15, and the three fractions $\frac{1}{4}$, $\frac{1}{2}$, $\frac{3}{4}$. Then divide the third column of the table into the fame number of

2

of equal parts, and in them write the same numbers likewife *.

The pulley C muft be placed above the table, and over it muft run the ftring, at the end of which is to hang the weight D, fufficiently heavy to keep it diftended, but not to put the pulley on the table in motion. To this ftring muft alfo be annexed the wire or index E, which muft be moveable, that it may be adapted to the unavoidable contraction or dilation of the ftring, occafioned by the moifture or dryness of the air : as otherwife it would not conftantly anfwer to the divifions on the board.

Provide a copper bafon, quite thin, about a foot in diameter, and one inch and a half deep. It fhould have two handles, that

* You may have other circles, on which may be wrote the 21 chances on the dice ; a number of anfwers to certain queftions, and a great variety of other matters ; as every one's fancy will fuggeft.

you

you may take it readily off the table without spilling the water. This bason is to go into each of the circles described above. Each of those circles also must have a private mark, by which you may place it on the table in its proper position.

Then, of very light wood or cork, make a small figure, in the shape of a siren or mermaid, in which is to be placed a magnetic bar, in a proper direction with regard to the magnetic horse-shoe. This figure is to float upon the surface of the water in the bason *.

In the last place, part of the step at the bottom of the frame must be moveable, in the manner of a lever, and communicate with the other side of the partition, so as to be visible to the person behind it, but not to any one in the room where the machine stands.

* Instead of a siren you may form a small fish of very thin copper, and hollow; or a small boat, or any other figure you please.

Now

Now, matters being thus prepared, when you place the bafon on the table in one of the circles, fo that its center is over the axis that turns the magnetic piece concealed in the table, if the perfon behind the partition draw the index in the ftring up to any one of the numbers, letters, or words on Pl. XV. the magnetic piece on the table will place itfelf againft the fame number, letter, or word. Therefore, if you place the firen on the furface of the water, it will, by means of the magnetic wire concealed in it, direct itfelf to that part where the large bar or horfe-fhoe is moved. If the perfon behind the partition draw the wire up and down, before he fix it, the firen will in like manner make various motions, as if undetermined where to fix.

RECREATION XLVI.

To make the firen of the magnetic table
point to all the letters of a given word.

YOU muſt have three cards, on which
are wrote the names of three perſons
or cities, or any other words you pleaſe.
One of theſe cards muſt be of the common ſize, another a little longer, and the
third a little wider.   Theſe cards you give
to any perſon and deſire him to chooſe
which of them he thinks proper, and to
keep it to himſelf.   He is then to return
you the two remaining cards, and you
will diſcover immediately, by the touch,
which card he has choſe.   You are pre-
viouſly to agree with the perſon behind the
partition on the three different expreſſions,
which denote the card that is choſen.   For
example, you are to ſay either, *The firen*
ſhall name the word; or *ſhe ſhall point to*
the letters that compoſe the word; or *ſhe*
will

will find out the word. Then your confederate, after giving the firen fome inde-
terminate motions, will direct her fucceffively to the feveral letters that compofe
the word wrote on the card.

Note, the confederate muft be of a
ready apprehenfion ; and to affift his me-
mory, adjoining to the forementioned table, he fhould have a paper, on which are
wrote the feveral figns you are to give
him.

The firen is to point out the time expreffed
by any given watch.

You defire any perfon to lend you his
watch, and laying it on the table, you tell
him that the firen fhall fhow the precife
time at which it then is. You then mount
the ftep, as if to place the watch more properly ; and at the fame time prefs down the
moveable piece as many times as are equal
to the hours. The perfon behind the par-

O 2

tition

tition obferving carefully that number, makes the firen point to it. You then make a fimilar fignal for the quarters and minutes, and your confederate, in like manner as before, makes the firen point refpectively to them.

To make the firen point to three numbers that have been chofen by three different perfons.

You muft have a fmall bag, like that defcribed in the 32d Recreation of this volume, in which there are four divifions. In the firft of them you muft put the numbers from 1 to 15; and in each of the three others feveral tickets that have the fame number, but not higher than 15. You draw out a handful of tickets from the firft divifion, and fhow that they confift of different numbers. Then put them again in that divifion, and offer one of the other divifions to the three perfons, from which they are each to draw a fingle number.

number. Your confederate being previoufly informed what thofe three numbers are, and in what order they are to be drawn, will immediately direct the firen to them.

After the parties have drawn the three numbers, you may afk whether the firen fhall point to their numbers feparately, or to the amount of the whole. Suppofe, for example, the three numbers be 5, 7, and 11, The firen is then made to point firft to 2, and then to 3, which form 23, the amount of thofe numbers.

You may likewife let the fame perfon draw two or three numbers, and the firen fhall fhow him either thofe numbers feparately, their amount, or their product when multiplied together.

A per-

A person having drawn a card from the pack, the siren points to the name of that card on the circle.

The person having drawn, from a piquet pack, the card that you have previously agreed on with your confederate, by your presenting that card in the manner already described, he immediately directs the siren to that card. It will be proper to agree on a second card with your confederate, that you may repeat the experiment if it should be desired.

A question being proposed by any person, the siren gives the answer; tho' the person who exhibits the recreation does not know the question.

On five cards write five such different questions as may be all answered by the same word: as for example.

1. What can be in all parts of the earth at the same time?

2. What

2. What does the ivy round the oak?

3. What muſt a man have to carry him crofs the ocean?

4. What is it the hunter does with his horn?

5. What makes a great noiſe but no fhow?

6. What brings trees, towers and fteeples to the ground?

All theſe queſtions are to be anſwered by the word *wind*. You therefore fhow that the cards contain different queſtions, and then give them to any perſon, telling him to chooſe one of them privately, and, keeping it to himſelf, to put the reſt in his pocket; which being done, your confederate directs the firen to the letters that compoſe that word. If you would repeat the experiment, you muſt have another fet of cards which have a different anſwer, that it may not appear that the fame word anſwers all the cards. This recreation is

eaſily

eafily performed, and occafions no fmall degree of furprife.

The principal part of thefe recreations with the firen were invented by M. Guyot, and were therefore never exhibited in public before the appearance of his book.

RECREATION XLVII.

The fagacious fwan.

PROVIDE a box X Y, (Pl. XVI. Fig. 1.) eighteen inches long, nine wide, and two deep, the top of which is to flide on and off, at the end Y. Toward the end X, defcribe a circle of fix inches diameter, round which are to be fixed fix fmall vafes of wood or ivory, of one inch and a half high; and to each of them there muft be a cover.

At the end Y place an egg B, of ivory or other matter, of about three inches and
a half

a half high, with a cover that fhuts by a hing, and faftens with a fpring. It muft be fixed on the ftand C, through which, as well as the bottom of the egg, and the part of the box directly underneath, there muft pafs a hole of one-third of an inch in diameter. In this cavity place an ivory cylinder F, that can move freely, and rifes or falls by means of the fpring R. You muft have a thin copper bafon A, of fix inches diameter, which is to be placed on the center of the circle at X, and confe-quently in the middle of the fix vafes.

Let a proper workman conftruct the movement expreffed by Fig. 2. which is compofed of a quadrant G, that has 16 teeth, and is moveable about an axis in the ftand H, that has an elbow, by which it is fcrewed to the bottom of the box at L. To the quadrant there muft be joined the ftrait piece K. The horizontal wheel M, has 24 teeth, and is fupported by the piece S, which is fcrewed to the end of the box

box next Y. On the axis of this wheel place a brafs rod O P, five inches long, and at the part O place a large bar or horfe-fhoe, of a femicircular form, and about two inches and a half diameter, ftrongly impregnated. The fteel rod V, takes at one end the teeth of the quadrant G, by the pinion F, and at the other end the wheel M, by the perpendicular wheel N, of 30 teeth ; the two ends of this rod are fupported by the two ftands that hold the other pieces. Under the piece K, that joins to the quadrant, muft be placed the fpring R, by which it is raifed, and pufhes up the cylinder that goes through the ftand C into the egg.

You muft alfo have fix fmall etwees or cafes as Y, Fig. 3. They muft be of the fame circumference with the cylinder in the ftand, and round at their extremities : their length muft be different, that when they are placed in the egg, and the lower end enters

enters the hole in which is the cylinder, they may thruft it down more or lefs, when the top of the egg, againft which they prefs, is faftened down; and thereby lower the bar that is fixed to the end of the qua-drant, and confequently, by means of the pinion F, and wheels N, M, turn the horfe-fhoe that is placed upon the axis of the laft wheel *.

In each of thefe etwees place a different queftion, wrote on a flip of paper and roll-ed up, and in each of the vafes put the anfwer to one of the queftions; as you will know, by trials, where the magnetic bar or horfefhoe will ftop.

Laftly, provide a fmall figure of a fwan, or what other you pleafe, made of cork or enamel, in which you muft fix a touched needle, of the largeft fize of thofe com-monly ufed in fewing.

* Thefe exact length of thefe etwees can be determined by trials only; which trials, however, may be made with round pieces of wood.

2   Being

Being thus prepared, you offer a perfon the fix etwees, and defire him to choofe any one of them himfelf, and conceal the others, or give them to different perfons. He is then to open his etwee, read the queftion it contains to himfelf, and return the etwee to you, after replacing the quef-tion. You then put the etwee in the egg, and placing the fwan upon the water in the bafon, you tell the company fhe will pre-fently difcover in which of the vafes the anfwer is contained. The fame experi-ment may be repeated with all the etwees.

This apparatus is more commodious than that of the firen, as it may be eafily moved from one place to another, and as there is here no occafion for a confederate. But at the fame time it will not admit of fo great a variety of experiments.

PLATE XVI

202.

J. Lodge Sc.

CONSTRUCTION OF THE COMMUNICA-
TIVE BELL.

LET there be made a box of copper in the form of part of a hollow covered cylinder, as A B (Pl. XVII. Fig. 1.) This box muft be placed upon the circle of wood C, that has at its center a pivot, on which is to be placed a touched needle D, three inches long, and thicker than the common needles; at each end it muft have a very fmall brafs knob, and near to one end of it there muft be placed a fmall bell, like that of a repeating watch; the bottom of this box muft be clofed with a gauze, that the needle may not be vifible.

On the infide of the magnetic table, Pl. XIV. place a double bar M O, of about five inches long, ftrongly impregnated, and fixed on an axis, under which is placed a double pulley of an inch diameter. To one part of this pulley fix a fmall cord, the other end being faftened to the fpring N. From

From the other part of the pulley muſt go a cord that paſſes over another pulley at A, and from thence, through the leg H, and behind the partition W ; in the ſame manner as in the experiment of the ſiren.

The motion of this cord being conſtantly the ſame, and of very little extent, a lever may be fixed behind the partition, by which the magnetic bar may be readily moved from B to C.

This preparation being made, when you place the copper box or cylinder on the table, in ſuch manner that the pivot which holds the needle is directly over that which holds the magnetic bar in the table *, if the lever behind the partition be thruſt down, the bar will be moved from B to C, and will cauſe the ſame motion in the needle, and conſequently make it ſtrike againſt the bell in the cylinder.

* There muſt be a mark on the cylinder, by which you will be directed in placing it on the table.

RECREATION XLVIII.

*To tell, by the communicative bell, the card
that a perfon has drawn from the pack.*

YOU are firft to obferve, that the
founding of the bell fignifies *yes*, and
its filence *no*.

Open the pack before the perfon, and
dextroufly prefent that card to him which
you have agreed on with your confederate.   When the perfon has drawn that
card you interrogate the bell, after the
following   manner.   Suppofe the card
drawn to be the knave of fpades.

Queftions.	Anfwers.
Do you know the perfon that has drawn the card?	Yes.
Is it a gentleman ?	No.
Is it a lady ?	Yes.
Do you know her ?	Yes.
Is fhe handfome ?	Yes.

Are

Queſtions.	Anſwers.
Are you ſure you know the card?	Yes.
Is it a diamond—a heart—a club?	No.
Are you ſure you are not miſtaken?	Yes.
Is it then a ſpade?	Yes.
Is it the king—ten—nine of ſpades?	No.
Is it the knave?	Yes.

This manner of anſwering queſtions may be applied to various intentions; as to naming the hour, or the number of perſons in company, &c. The foregoing Recreation is ſufficiently common; the following is ſomething more extraordinary.

To tell, by the bell, at what number, from the top, any card of a pack is, that a perſon ſhall name.

To perform this Recreation you muſt be provided with a piquet pack of cards, in which the ſeveral ſuites are placed in
the

the following order, diamonds, fpades, hearts, and clubs: and the cards of every fuite in their natural rank, as ace, king, queen, knave, ten, &c.

You fhuffle them, according to the manner prefcribed in p. 79. of the firft volume, and they will then be in the following order.

1	Knave	} clubs	17	Eight diamonds	
2	Ten		18	King	
3	Eight		19	Queen	
4	Seven	} hearts	20	Knave	} fpades
5	King		21	Eight	
6	Queen		22	Seven	
7	Ten	} fpades	23	Ace	
8	Nine		24	Knave	} hearts
9	Seven diamonds		25	Ten	
10	Ace fpades		26	Nine	
11	Queen		27	Ace	
12	Knave		28	King	
13	Ace	} diamonds	29	Queen	} clubs
14	King		30	Nine	
15	Ten		31	Eight	
16	Nine		32	Seven	

A copy of this arrangement your confederate muſt have. Therefore when the perſon has named the card he chooſes, he who is behind the partition hearing what card it is, either by the other's naming it, or your repeating it, by looking on his ſcheme will ſee the number at which it is placed, and immediately ſtrike that number on the bell.

This Recreation is the more extraordinary, as it may be repeated a ſecond or third time, by your ſhuffling the cards in a determinate order; nothing more being neceſſary than for the confederate to have a ſcheme of the ſituation of the cards after each ſhuffle.

RECRE-

RECREATION XLIX.

The magnetic balance.

YOU muſt have a ſmall balance, ſuch as is commonly uſed for weighing money, as A B (Plate XVII. Fig. 2.) It ſhould be very exact, and the ſcales muſt be iron or ſteel, very thin, and gilt or laquered. This balance muſt be ſupported by a ſtand fixed to the top of the magnetic table. The bottom of the ſcales ſhould not be above half an inch diſtant from the table.

You muſt obſerve, that they are to be placed over that part of the table where is the magnetic bar that is uſed for the firen and bell : ſo that the centers of the two ſcales are to be over the points O and M. Theſe ſcales muſt be ſtrongly touched, that they may be the more eaſily attracted by the magnetic bar.

P 2

This

This preparation being made, you afk a perfon to lend you two pieces of money, fuppofe two guineas, and you place them in the fcales, which will remain in equilibrium, if the pieces be of equal weight. You then propofe to the perfon to augment the weight of either of them at pleafure, and when he has determined, your confederate behind the partition, by means of the lever, moves the bar toward one of the fcales, and it immediately defcends. You then, if required, make the fame experiment with the other fcale.

To give your confederate notice which fcale is to be moved, nothing more is neceffary than to fay, is it *this*, or is it *that* fcale; you having previoufly agreed with him which fcale the words *this* or *that* fhall fignify.

SECRE-

RECREATION L.

The sympathetic dials.

LET there be two dials conſtructed of the ſame form and ſize. The movements of each conſiſting of a barrel A, and the four wheels A, B, C, D, with their pinions, and the fly F. The ſame as in the ſtriking part of a clock or dial, (See Pl. XVII. Fig. 3.)

The movements of each of them muſt be encloſed between two plates of braſs G and H, Fig. 4. of about two inches and a half diameter, and diſtant from each other about two-thirds of an inch. Let the axis of the wheel C paſs through the center of the upper plate G, which is to be covered with a dial plate, that ſerves for ornament only. On the ſame axis place a needle or index, as in a common dial.

Under

Under the plate H, Fig. 3. and on the axis of the barrel, continued out beyond the plate, fix a wheel with a catch, by which the movement of each of the dials may be wound up.

To one of thefe dials let there be a catch or trigger on the outfide, by which it may be ftopped or put in motion with a touch of the finger. To the other dial fix the catch L N M, whofe axis is at N ; the end L takes the fly of the movement, and confequently when the other end is thruft back the wheels are at liberty to move. This catch is to be placed on the brafs wheel H, near the part I. It is to be of fteel, well polifhed and touched, with its fouth pole at M. Great care muft be taken to make this part move extremely free, that it may be eafily attracted by the bar in the magnetic table, on which it is to be placed. Each of thefe dials is to be enclofed in a cafe of thin copper or brafs Q R.

Qq

On the infide of the magnetic table, Plate XIV. place the piece O P, compofed of four fteel bars ftrongly impregnated: they fhould be feven or eight inches long, half an inch wide, and one inch thick: they muft be bound clofe together by four brafs rings, of which that next P fhould be larger than the reft, and ftanding out beyond the bars, fhould have a hole thro' it, by which it is to be fixed on a pivot at P. Thefe bars are to be drawn toward N, where they are to be ftopped by the fpring R. There muft alfo be a ftring, which, pafling over the pullies S and T, goes down the leg of the table; the bottom of which is to be a lever or treddle, under the ftep, by means of which the piece O P may be moved by your foot.

You therefore place the fecond dial on the table, directly over that part where the extremity of the bars O P is; when you put your foot upon the lever at the

bottom

bottom of the table. Therefore if you then place your foot on that lever, the bars attracting the end M, of the catch, will fet the fly at liberty, and the wheels being put in motion, the index on the front of the dial will move with confiderable velocity; but when you take your foot off the lever, the catch will again take the fly, and ftop the movement.

Therefore having placed the fecond dial as above directed, you give the other dial, that had the end of the catch on the outfide, to any perfon, and tell him, that when he fhall ftop it, or put it in motion, the dial on the table will, by fympathy, do the fame, and by mounting the ftep you make it perform accordingly. You may alfo tell him that the dial on the table fhall either ftop or go, at his command : but this perhaps may deftroy the notion of the dials acting by fympathy.

You

You may contrive to have ftops or le-
vers at different parts of the room, by car-
rying the cord under the floor : or in an
adjacent room, to be moved by a confederate.

CONSTRUCTION OF THE MAGNETIC ROLLER.

PROVIDE a board two feet and a half
long, three inches and a half wide,
and half an inch thick, (fee Plate XVII.
Fig. 5.) and divide it into ten equal parts,
in each of which defcribe a circle, and divide its circumference likewife into ten
equal parts. In each of the circles make
a groove, and in each groove place a magnetic bar, whofe poles are to be difpofed
as in the figure. Under each end of the
board place a roller, on which it is to move
in the magnetic table, Plate XIV.

To the end A of the roller (fee Pl. XIV.)
faften a cord, which is to pafs over a pulley
at B, and go down the leg of the table:

to

to the end of this cord is to be faftened a weight, inclofed in a bag, which is to pafs freely up and down the hole at B.   To the other end B, of the roller, there muft like-wife be faftened a cord, which, paffing over a pulley at A, going down the leg of the table, and through the ftep at the bottom, comes out behind the partition W.

Againft the other fide of the partition place the table in page 220 ; and at the top of it fix a pulley, over which muft pafs a ftring, with a weight at the end, and to the ftring muft be faftened an index ; as in the experiment of the firen.

The table is formed in the following manner.   You are firft to determine by trials, the fpace that the index faftened to the ftring paffes over, while each of the ten divifions of the roller comes to the point S, in the magnetic table ; and mark them down on the plan.   Then divide it into five columns.   In the ten divifions of the firft column write the numbers 10, 9, 8, 7, 6, 5, 4, 3, 2, 1. In the ten divifions of the fecond column write the vowels A, E, I, O, U, and the five confonants D, G, L, N, R. In the divifions of the third column write the figures 1, 2, 3, 4, 5, 6, 7, 8, 9, 0. In the fourth column, in every other divifion, write the name of one of the five following cards, ace of fpades, eight of fpades, feven of fpades, nine of hearts, feven of hearts. In the fifth column write, after the fame manner, the names of five ftates, as England, Portugal, Spain, Pruffia, Auftria. You may place what other letters you pleafe in the fecond column, but they fhould be fuch as by their combinations will produce feveral words. The words in the fourth and fifth columns may likewife be changed for fuch as will anfwer to any other queftions you choofe.

TABLE

TABLE.

Divisions	Letters	Figures	Cards	States
10	A	1	ace spades	
9	E	2		England
8	I	3	8 spades	
7	O	4		Portugal
6	U	5	7 spades	
5	D	6		Spain
4	G	7	9 hearts	
3	L	8		Prussia
2	N	9	7 hearts	
1	R	0		Austria

Now it follows from what has been said, that when the person behind the partition fixes the index in the cord against any one of these divisions, the part of the roller which corresponds to that division will be brought opposite to the point S, in the magnetic table, and consequently the touched needles in the pieces hereafter described, will place themselves in the same direction with the bar in that part of the roller.

THE

RECREATION LI.

The magician's box.

FIRST conftruct the bafe A B, (Plate XVIII. Fig. 1.) of fix inches long, four wide, and one deep. Let it be hollow, and covered with a piece Q, that flides in in a groove. In the middle of the top piece make a hole, either fquare or round, of about half an inch wide.

On this bafis place four planes of glafs F, Fig. 2. joined together in the form of a truncated pyramid, and lined with gauze, or thin paper. At its bottom I L, it fhould be two inches and a half fquare, but at top only one inch and a half. At the opening place a convex glafs V, of five inches focus, that is, equal to the height of the machine. Let it be fixed to the bafe A B.

On the infide of the bafe, and at two inches diftance from one of its fhorteft fides, fix a pivot, on which is to be placed
the

the circle of pasteboard O P, Fig. 3. of four inches diameter, in which must be fixed the touched needle Q R. The pasteboard circle must be divided into ten equal parts, as in the figure; which parts are to correspond to the divisions in the foregoing table. In the five divisions 1, 3, 5, 7, 9, are to be drawn the cards there expressed.

On a second circle of pasteboard, that has the same divisions, write in those marked 2, 4, 6, 8, 10, the five names of different states mentioned in the foregoing table.

As each circle must be previously placed on the base, and changed for every different recreation, it will be proper to have two boxes, as it would be impolitic to change the circles before the spectators. It would be still much better if the box could be placed in a chest or cabinet, that was fixed against a partition, behind which

which a confederate is placed; for then, after performing one recreation, the box might be placed in the cabinet, and the confederate, by a private opening in the partition, might take out the circle, and infert another.

It will be eafy to conceive, from what has been already faid, that when the machine is placed on the magnetic table, at the part S, fo that the pivot on which the circle turns is exactly over the point S; the bar in the part of the roller then there, will put the needle in a fimilar direction, and confequently by looking into the machine, the fpectator will fee the card, letter, or word, that is oppofite the index in the table of columns.

A per-

A person is to name the state in which is the
city whose name is on the cards that
have been dealt to another.

On thirty cards write the names of the
five following cities; London, Lisbon, Ma-
drid, Berlin, Vienna.   Then shuffle and
deal them after the manner explained in
page 79. of the first volume.

Then tell the second person to look
into the box, and read the name of the
state in which is the city whose name is
on the cards in the first person's hand.
The same is to be done for the four other
parties.

To perform this Recreation, nothing
more is necessary than to have a circle
with the names of the five states; and that
the confederate be instructed in the order
that each name is to be brought forward to
the eye of the spectator.

In

In recreations of this kind it will be proper to have a hole in the partition, by which the confederate will know when to move the circle, and keep it steady till he who performs the experiment has covered the eye-glass of the box.

RECREATION LII.

The mystical dial.

PROVIDE a board four inches square, and let it be supported at the four corners by feet about one quarter of an inch high, as A B (Plate XVIII. Fig. 4.) On this board draw two concentric circles, and divide them into ten equal parts, in nine of which write one of the numbers from 1 to 9, and in the tenth an o. These numbers muft be placed in the fame manner as in the figure, and the line A B muft divide the divifions marked 1 and 6, into two equal parts. At the center of this dial place a needle of a convenient fize.

It is evident from the construction of this dial, that when the person behind the partition places the index of his table against any number in the third column, the needle of this dial, when it is placed over the roller in the magnetic table, will point to the same number.

To show, by the foregoing dial, the numbers that two persons have chose, their sum, or their product.

You must here have the small bag described in p. 140: in the first division of which put the numbers from 1 to 10, and in three other divisions any numbers you please, suppose 3, 7, and 8; that is, all the tickets in each of those three divisions must have the same number. You then offer two different divisions of the bag to two persons, and they each draw one number, suppose 5 and 7, you having previously agreed with your confederate what the numbers are to be.

You

You then afk them whether the index fhall point to their numbers fucceffively, their amount, or their product when multiplied together.

If the numbers are to appear fingly, the confederate firft directs the index of his table to the number 5, which you are to allow him a fufficient time to do. You then place the index on the dial, and turning it about it will ftop at that number. You take off the index while your confederate moves the flider, and placing it on again it will then ftop at 7.

If the amount of the two numbers be required, the confederate directs his index firft to 1 and then to 2, which make 12. If the product be required, he directs the needle, in like manner, firft to 3 and then to 5, which make 35.

You muft obferve to take the needle off the pivot immediately after it ftops, before

Q 2

fore

fore the roller begins to move again: and as the needle will place itfelf directly in the pofition of the bar underneath, you muft turn it about as foon as you have placed it on the pivot. Attention fhould be had to this obfervation in all the experiments with the magnetic needle.

RECREATION LIII.

The magical game of all-fours.

TO perform this Recreation you muft have a pafteboard circle, on which there are twelve divifions, on fix of which cards are to be painted, and to which fix divifions of the roller muft be adapted. A pack of cards are to be previoufly ranged and fhuffled, after the manner defcribed in the firft volume, p. 78. and when they are dealt, the hands are to be as follows.

Eldeft

Eldeft		Youngeft	
King	} fpades	Ace	
Ten		Queen	} fpades
Ace clubs		Nine	
Ace diamonds		Ace	
King	} hearts	Queen	} hearts
Knave		Eight	

Turn–up card, knave of fpades.

The eldeft takes up his cards. Thofe dealt for the youngeft lie on the table. Now the natural way of playing the above cards would be as follows : firft, the eldeft hand would lead one of his aces, which the youngeft would win with his nine of trumps ; and then play his ace and queen of hearts, the latter of which the eldeft would win with his king : he would next lead his other ace, to which the youngeft would play his eight of hearts. The eldeft muft then lead from his king and ten of trumps, both which the youngeft muft take with his ace and queen, and confe-quently have higheft, loweft, and game,

Q 3 which,

which, with the knave turned up, will make him all-fours.

Therefore when the eldeſt plays, you ſay aloud to another perſon, the gentleman plays the ace of clubs, for example, look in the box and ſee what card I muſt play; when your confederate will directly bring the nine of trumps on the circle to view. When it is your turn to play, you have no occaſion to ſay any thing, but only deſire the perſon to look in the box and ſee what card is played, your confederate having directions what to do. Thus you go on till the eldeſt has played all his cards. But you muſt obſerve, each time the circle is to be moved to prevent the perſon from immediately looking into the box, by ſome amuſing diſcourſe; or it might be better to ſtand by the box yourſelf, in order to cover and uncover it each time the perſon is to look in, that the circle may have time to ſettle.

RECREATION LIV.

The intelligent fly.

AT the center of a box about six inches
square and one inch deep (Pl. XVIII.
Fig. 5.) place a pivot.   Have a touched
needle L, three inches and a half long,
and at the end of it that is touched fix a
fly made of enamel : the other end of the
needle muft be fomething heavier, to keep
it in equilibrium.   This needle is to be
placed on the pivot.

On a piece of fquare pafteboard that will
juft go into the box, draw a circle, ABCD,
three inches and a half diameter; and an—
other at a fmall diftance, concentric with
the former.   The part within the laft
circle muft be cut out.   This pafteboard
circle is to be placed about half an inch
from the bottom of the box, and divided
into ten equal parts, in which are to be

Q 4   wrote

wrote the letters A, E, I, O, U, D, G, L, N, R, as in the figure.

Place a glafs about half an inch above the circle, and cover it with a circle of paper C, large enough to hide the needle, and leave only the fly vifible ; on this paper you may paint fome allegoric figures, that its ufe may not be fufpected. You muft next write on 24 cards the following queftions. Thefe cards are to be packed and fhuffled, according to the method explained in the firft volume, p. 78. that they may be in the order the queftions are here placed.

QUESTIONS.

1. Which is the land of liberty ? 2. Which is the firft city in the world ? 3. Whom do many men defpife, though they have not half his merit ? 4. Who is the pooreft man in the world? 5. Who is the meaneft of all mankind ? 6. For what do all young women long ? 7. Who, by ftation, is the
moft

3

4

moſt miſerable of all beings. 8. By what does a man diſcover his weakneſs? 9. What would every married woman do if ſhe could? 10. In what does a man ſhow his pride and folly? 11. What makes a woman cry more than the loſs of her huſband? 12. How does a man talk who has nothing to ſay? 13. What moſt reſembles a fine lady? 14. What frequently reminds us of a great loſs, without giving diſguſt? 15. What makes a young woman in love with an old man? 16. What does the poet want to cover his empty ſkull? 17. What ſhould a man never take from the woman he loves? 18. What muſt that man be who would gain the eſteem of all? 19. Who is he that ſeeks a man's company when his money and friends are all gone? 20. What gains the good will of the phyſician, the lawyer, and the harlot? 21. What do good men revere and knaves abuſe? 22. What does a man depend on when he truſts to his friends for ſupport? 23. What

23. What can he be sure of, who leaves his affairs to other ? 24. What makes as great a difference almost, if not altogether, between this man and that, as between that and a brute ?

After you have ranged the cards in the manner before mentioned, you place them on the table, and aſk any perſon which of them, in the order they then ſtand, ſhall contain the queſtion to which the fly ſhall give him the anſwer. If he ſay, for example, the 20th, your confederate, who has the following copy of the anſwers, will make the needle, at the end of which the fly is, ſucceſſively point to the letters that compoſe that word: then counting the cards over till you come to the 20th, you will find that word anſwer the queſtion.

A N S W E R S.

1. England.   2. London.   3. A dog.
4. A niggard.   5. A liar.   6. A ring.
7. A

7. A nun. 8. Anger. 9. Rule. 10. A duel. 11. An onion. 12, Loud. 13. An angel. 14. A dial. 15. Gold. 16. A laurel. 17. A denial. 18. Generous. 19. A dunn. 20. A guinea. 21. Religion. 22. A reed. 23. Ruin. 24. Learning.

Many other recreations may be performed by this intelligent fly by numbers, cards, &c. fimilar to thofe we have already explained on other occafions, and which, to avoid the appearance of repetition, we fhall not here defcribe.

RECREATION LV.

The multifarious verse.

THE eight words that compose this Latin verse,

Tot sunt tibi dotes quot cæli sidera virgo *.

being privately placed in any one of the different combinations, of which they are susceptible, and which are 40,320 in number, to tell the order in which they are placed.

Provide a box that shuts with hinges, and is eight inches long, three wide, and half an inch deep (Plate XIX. Fig. 1.) Have eight pieces of wood about one-third of an inch thick, two inches long, and one and a half wide, which will therefore, when placed close together, exactly fill

* Thy virtues, virgin, are as numerous as the stars of heaven.

the

the box. In each of these pieces or tablets place a magnetic bar, with their poles as is expressed in the figure. The bars being covered over, write on each of the tablets, in the order they then stand, one of the words of the foregoing Latin verse.

On a very thin board of the same dimension with the box, Fig. 2, draw the eight circles, A, B, C, D, E, F, G, H, whose centers should be exactly over those of the eight tablets in the box, when the board is placed upon it. Divide each of those circles into eight parts, as in the figure, and in each of those divisions write one of the words of the Latin verse, and in the precise order expressed in the plate, so that when the board is placed over the box, the eight touched needles placed at the center of the circles may be regulated by the poles of the bars in the box, and consequently the word that the needle points to in the circle be the same with that inscribed on the tablet. Cover the board with a

glafs

glaſs to prevent the needles from riſing off their pivots, as is done in the ſea-compaſs.

Over the board place four plates of glaſs, I, L, M, N, Fig. 3, which will give the machine the figure of a truncated pyramid, of eight inches high. Cover it with a glaſs, or rather a board in which are placed two lenſes of eight inches focus, and diſtant from each other about half an inch. Line the four plates of glaſs that compoſe the ſides with very thin paper, that will admit the light, and at the ſame time prevent the company from ſeeing the circles on the board.

Theſe preparations being made, you give the box to any one, and tell him to place the tablets on which the words are wrote, privately, in what poſition he thinks proper, then to cloſe the box, and if he pleaſe, to wrap it up in paper, ſeal it, and give it you. Then placing the board with the pyramid upon it, you immediately tell
him

him the order in which the tablets are placed, by reading the words to which the needles on the circles point.

This Recreation, which appears to have been invented by M. Guyot, is of the fame nature with that of the box of numbers, that has been frequently exhibited, but much more entertaining. For here there is not only a vaft number of combinations to be formed, but the words at the fame time conftantly preferve ohe meaning. If the firft inventors of this fort of recreation had made ufe of words in this manner, inftead of numbers, the inveftigation would have been attended with much more difficulty.

RECREATION LVI.

The communicative mirror.

LET there be made a box A B, (Plate XX. Fig. 1.) the top of which draws off at the end A. Let it be on the infide nine inches long, fix wide, and two-thirds of an inch deep. At the bottom of this box, and at three inches diftance from the end A, fix a pivot, on which is to be placed the circle of pafteboard M, Fig. 2. that contains a touched needle. Divide this circle into four equal parts, in three of which paint three cards, in the pofition exprefled in the figure.

In the top of the box make a hole an inch and half in diameter, over which place the pedeftal C D, compofed of four plates of glafs, covered on the infide with very thin paper.

On

On the top of the pedeftal place the tube
E F, about fix inches long and one and a
half in diameter. In this tube, at M, is to
be fixed an inclined mirror, by which the
part of the pafteboard circle under the
hole at L, may be feen by the eye at G.
At the end F of the tube place an eye-
glafs, whofe focus is equal to the diftance
G M ; and at the end E, any glafs you
pleafe. At the end B of the box, place
the mirror T V, which ferves to make the
fpectator think it is in that he fees the
card on the pafteboard.

In the box A B C D, Fig. 3. that fhuts
with hinges, and is of the fame dimenfion
with the infide of the other box, are to be
placed fucceffively the three tablets X, Y, Z,
in one determinate pofition. In each of
thefe tablets muft be fixed a magnetic bar,
in the manner expreffed in the figure, and
on each of them is to be pafted one of the
fame cards with thofe on the pafteboard

circle. One of these tablets, as, for example, that marked Z, being placed in the box, in the manner expressed in the third figure, the needle on the circle will place itself in a corresponding position, and the similar card on the circle will come under the pedestal. You therefore present the box, Fig. 3. and the three tablets, to a person, desiring him to place any one of them he thinks proper, in the box, privately; then to conceal the others, and after he has closed the box, to return it you. Then, placing the first box with the pedestal, tube, and mirror over the other, you direct him to look in the seeming perspective-glass, when he will see the figure of the card he placed in the box, and it will appear to him to be in the mirror C V.

You may have a fourth tablet, that contains a bar, but on which there is nothing painted. This tablet you may place first
in

in the box, and let the party fee that when there is no card in the box he cannot fee any in the perfpective.

RECREATION LVII.

The box of dice by reflection.

LET there a fmall box of wood, A B C D, (Plate XX. Fig. 4.) ten inches long, two wide, and one and a half high. At the two ends of this box fix the two hollow cubes I, L, one inch and a half fquare, in which are to be placed two dice exactly of the fame dimenfion.

The ends A C and B D of the box are to have fliders that draw up, in the manner expreffed by Fig. 5. There muft be likewife at each end a fmall pannel M, that may be raifed or depreffed one-tenth of an inch, by which

a fmall

a fmall hole at N may be covered or uncovered; and through this hole you are to fee into the box.

The top and two longeft fides of the box are to be of glafs, lined with a thin paper. Within the box are to be placed two mirrors O P and Q R, at an angle of forty-five degrees, by which, when you look through the holes at the two ends of the box, you will eafily fee the bottoms of the two cubes I, L, that are placed on it.

Divide the bottoms of the cubes juft mentioned into four equal parts, by diagonals drawn from the oppofite angles, as in Fig. 8. and again divide that fide next the middle of the box into fix equal parts, which are to correfpond to the fix points that are on a die.

Under each of the cubes place a fmall brafs ftand A B, Fig. 6. which is to be

dif-

difpofed as in Fig. 7. On the ftand there muft be a pivot, directly under the cen-- ter of the cube, and it muft hold two needles, one of brafs and the other of fteel, and touched. Thefe needles are to be placed at right angles to each other, as in the figure.

Divide each face of the die into four equal parts, by diagonals from the oppo- fite angles, and then divide each fide into fix equal parts, and in each fide of the die, oppofite to one of thofe parts, each different from the other, place a magnetic bar one inch and a quarter long, two- tenths of an inch wide, and one-tenth thick. All the divifions on thefe dice muft be very exact : cover them with double papers, and write on each fide of them the points it is to exprefs, when its op- pofite fide is next the touched needle : they are then to be placed in the two hollow cubes, which are to be covered.

R 3

This

This machine being conftructed with care, according to the foregoing directions, you prefent the two dice to any perfon, and defire him to place them privately in the two cubes, in what pofition he pleafe, and put on their covers. Then looking through the two holes, you immediately tell him, by the direction of the needles to the under fides of the cubes, the exact number of points they compofe.

THE

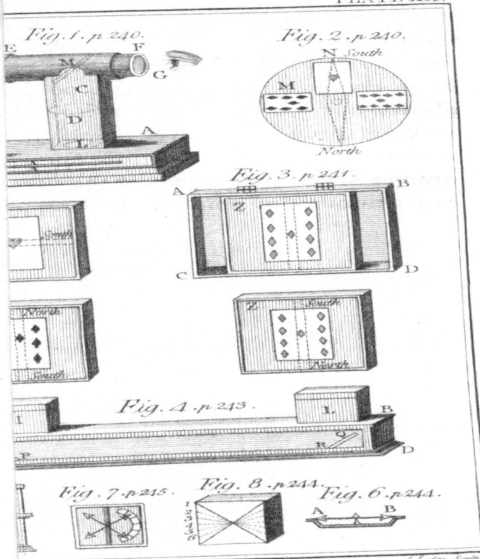

PLATE XX.

Fig. 1. p. 240.

Fig. 2. p. 240.

Fig. 3. p. 241.

Fig. 4. p. 243.

Fig. 7. p. 215.

Fig. 8. p. 244.

Fig. 6. p. 244.

J. Lodge Sculp.

THE
CONTENTS.

CONTENTS.

ELECTRICAL RECREATIONS.

Divided into ſuch as are performed in the light, and ſuch as require a dark chamber   p. 46

RECREATION I.   p. 46

The animated feather.

A feather being brought near an excited tube is firſt attracted by it and then repelled, and the tube cannot be brought
cloſe

close to the feather, till it has touched some other body.

RECREATION II.

The self-raising pyramid.

A large bundle of threads being suspended from the electric branch, (Plate IV. Fig. 3.) will rise up in form of a pyramid, and continue so as long as the wheel is turned, but when that ceases the threads will resume their first position.

RECREATION III.

The magical dance.

Three bells are suspended from the electric branch, and between them hang two brass knobs. The bells being electrified will attract the clappers, and be struck by them, and the ringing will continue as long as the machine is in motion. This is the music for the dance. A plate is then suspended from the branch,

150   CONTENTS.

branch, and on a metal ftand, placed
under it, are put the figures of men,
which being attracted by the plate will
be in continual motion. This Recreation may be fufpended or renewed at
pleafure.

RECREATION   IV.   p. 52

The artificial fpider.

The body of this fpider is of cork, and its
legs of linen thread.   When it is held,
by a fine line of filk, between the electric branch, and an excited ftick of wax,
it will appear to be animated, continually jumping from one to the other.

RECREATION   V.   p. 53

The marvellous fountain.

A veffel of water, in which a fyphon is
placed, being fufpended from the branch,
as foon as it is electrified the water will
begin to flow, and when the electrification

tion is ftrong feveral ftreams will iffue, in form of a cone. This experiment may be diverfified by ufing a fountain made with condenfed air.

RECREATON VI.   P. 54

The magic picture.

This picture or print muft have a frame and glafs. The border of the print is cut off, all round : the upper and under part of the middle of the glafs is covered with tin-foil, that communicates by the bottom of the frame : over this tin-foil the print is pafted. When the picture is a portrait a crown is placed on its head, which a ftranger attempting to take off, at the fame time he holds the frame by the bottom, receives a fmart fhock, and fails in the attempt.

R E C R E A T I O N   IX.   p. 62

The self-moving wheel.

This wheel is constructed on the same principle as the foregoing. A circular plate of glass, gilt on both sides, is fixed to a perpendicular axis : on the edge of this wheel are fixed two bullets, one communicating with the upper surface, and the other with the under surface ; twelve small pillars of glass, with a thimble on the top of each of them,

them, are fixed in a circular stand, round the wheel. When this wheel is well charged, the bullets on its edge being differently electrified, attract and repel the thimbles alternately, and thereby give the wheel a motion that increases continually, till it goes more than 20 turns in a minute, and the motion will continue half an hour. The celerity of this wheel may be increased by an additional number of bullets.

RECREATION X.   p. 65

The magician's chace.

A wire is placed perpendicular to the branch, and on the top of it turn several horizontal wires, the points of which are bent in opposite directions, and on them are fixed the figures of men, horses, hounds, &c. When these wires are electrified they will turn swiftly round, and the figures will seem to pursue each other. This Recreation may be improved by another set of wires,

placed

CONTENTS.

RECREATION XI.   p. 67

The planetarium.

Six concentric hoops of metal are fufpended from the branch ; under and near to them is placed a metal plate, on which are put glafs bubbles, between the hoops ; thefe bubbles correfpond to the planets, the hoops to their orbits, and a ball hung over the center of the hoops reprefents the fun. When the hoops are electrified the balls will move round them, and the motion will continue as long as the operator thinks fit.

RECREATION XII.   p. 69

The incendiaries.

A perfon ftanding on a cake of wax holds a chain that is connected with the branch, and putting his finger into a difh

difh containing fpirit of wine, it will
be immediately in a blaze; and if a
wick that communicates with the fpirit
be laid to a train of gunpowder, it may
blow up a magazine, or fet fire to a
city. This experiment may be diverfified by making the electricity pafs
through feveral perfons that touch each
other.

RECRÉATION XIII. p. 72

The inconceivable fhock.

A perfon holding a chain that is joined to
one of the hooks of the electric table,
attempts to fix a wire on the other hook,
when he inftantly receives a fhock
through the body, without knowing
from whence it proceeds. This Recreation may be diverfified by concealing
the chain under a carpet on which a
perfon treads, and by laying a wire
that communicates with the other
hook, in fuch manner that he may ac-
ciden-

tidentally take hold of it. Methods of communicating the fhock to a great number of perfons at the fame time

RECREATION XIV. p. 75

Magical explofions.

Gunpowder is made up in the form of a fmall cartridge, in each end of which is put a blunt wire; the ends of thefe wires within the cartridge are about half an inch diftant. Two chains, that communicate with the two hooks in the electric table, being joined to the external ends of the wires, the electric fire will pafs through the cartridge, with an inftant explofion. By a fimilar method brafs or iron wire may be melted.

RECREATION XV. p 78

Prifmatic colours.

A tin plate is placed between two wires that communicate with the two hooks

RECREATION XVI. p. 81

The artificial earthquake.

An edifice, compofed of feveral loofe
pieces, is placed on a board in the middle of a large bafon of water. A wire
that communicates with the hooks in
the table, being laid over the board and
the furface of the water, they become
greatly agitated by the explofion, and
the edifice is laid in ruins.

RECREATION XVII. p 82

The electrical kite.

This kite confifts of a large thin filk handkerchief, whofe corners are faftened to
the

the ends of two flips of cedar, and to
the top of the upright piece is fixed a
pointed wire, about a foot long : the
other parts are the fame as in a common
kite. To the end of the twine next the
hand a filk ribband is tied, and where
the twine and ribband join a key is
hung. This kite is raifed when thunder is approaching. The electricity is
conducted from the wire of the kite to
the twine, and from that to the key,
by which a phial may be charged and
all the common experiments in electricity performed. Account of fome
very extraordinary phenomena that
were produced by an electric kite in the

S 2   R E-

6

the

S 3 RECRE-

RECRE-

RECREATION XXIII. p. 101

The magical conftellations.

On a board are marked a number of fpots, at different diftances, fo as to correfpond with the ftars in two or more contiguous conftellations. On the fides of each fpot are made two holes, in which wires are placed, that nearly meet over the fpot. The other ends of the wires communicate with the branch, and when that is electrified all the ftars appear luminous, and fhine with unfading luftre as long as the machine is in motion.

RECREATION XXIV. p. 103

The luminous characters.

Several rows of tin-foil, that all communicate, are placed on a board, at equal diftances (Plate III. Fig. 1.) From

S 4

thefe

thefe rows the characters are cut out.
.. One end of the tin-foil being brought
to the conductor the electric fire would
pafs over the whole imperceptibly, but
being ftopped by the breaks in the lines
it jumps from one to the other, and
all the characters become luminous,
and remain fo as long as the operator
thinks fit.

Prifmatic illuminations.

An exhaufted cylinder is fixed to a lath,
and is rubbed by the hand as it turns,
when a body of light, variegated with
all the colours of a prifm, appears
in the glafs, and thefe colours are
continually changing. When a little
air is let into the cylinder the colours
are more vivid : when more air is ad-
mitted there are continual corrufcations,
with the appearance of a cafcade of fire,
trees, mofs, &c.

RECRE-

RECREATION XXVI. p. 108

The aurora borealis.

A Torricellian vacuum is made in a glaſs
tube, one end of which is applied to
the conductor, and the other end held
in the hand; the whole tube then appears to be filled with light, which
continues for a conſiderable time: after
this light diſappears, if the tube be
drawn through the hand, a very intenſe
light is ſeen, and reaches, without interruption, from one hand to the
other.

RECREATION XXVII. p. 110

The circulating lamps.

To the upper axis of the ſelf movingwheel
are fixed ſeveral radii, and from the
end of each of them hangs a lamp,
filled with ſpirit, and that of each lamp
is

is tinged with a different colour. The wheel having acquired a confiderable velocity is placed under the branch, from which hangs a chain, that as the wheel turns round dips into the fpirit of each lamp and fets it on fire. Thefe lamps being all of different colours, and revolving in a quick fucceffion, produce a pleafing effect.

MAGNETISM.

RECRE-

A large fewing-needle, that is ftrongly touched, is concealed in a crown piece. You defire a perfon to lend you a piece of the fame fort, which you change for the other, and giving that to the perfon, you difcover whether it be enclofed in a fnuff-box, or not, by holding the magnetic perfpective over the box.

A magnet is concealed under a table, and is moveable by a pin, at one end of it. Small nails are laid on that part of the table where the magnet then is, and they are attracted by a key you hold over them. You change the pofition of the magnet, by the pin, and give the key to any one, when it will

not

not attract the nails. You change the position of the magnet a second time, and giving the key to another perfon, it will immediately attract the nails.

The myfterious watch.

You afk any one to lend you his watch, and placing it over that part of the table mentioned in the laft Recreation, where the magnet is, it will prefently ftop. You change the pofition of the magnet, and defire the perfon to lay his watch in the fame place, when it will not ftop. You move the magnet a fecond time, and giving the watch to another perfon, it will ftop as before.

The bouquets.

A fmall box of thin wood (Pl VII. Fig. 1.) is contrived to contain two artificial flowers ;

flowers; the principal ftalk of each of them is ftrongly touched, but in different directions. By holding the magnetic perfpective over the box you difcover which of the flowers is concealed in it.

RECREATION XXXII. p. 139

The magnetic dial.

A magnetic needle is concealed in a hollow circle, (Plate VII. Fig. 2.) and oppofite its north end a pin is fixed in the border of the circle; over the needle is placed a dial, that moves freely in the hollow circle, and on which are numbers, &c. A perfon draws a ticket from a bag, in which there are feveral divifions, and then turning the hand of the dial about it ftops at the number he has drawn; you having previoufly fet the north end of the magnet, by the pin in the circle, to that number on the dial.

RECRE-

RECREATION XXXIII. p. 143

The magnetical cards.

This Recreation is fimilar to the laft, but
here inftead of the numbers of the
hours, one of each of the four fuits of
the cards are drawn, and the eight
names of the cards of piquet are wrote
(Plate VII. Fig. 4.) You offer a piquet
pack to a perfon that he may draw a
card, taking care that he draws the long
card, as is explained in the firft volume.
He then turns the needle round, and it
ftops at the card he drew; you having
previoufly placed the magnet againft
that card. This Recreation may be
diverfified by having two needles, and
letting two perfons draw each a different long card.

R E-

RECREATION XXXIV. p. 147

The dexterous painter.

There are two fmall boxes and four
fmall boards, (Plate VIII. Fig. 1.) on
which different fubjects are painted,
and in each of which a magnet is concealed. There is likewife a fmall circle
of pafteboard, Fig. 2, on which are drawn
the fame fubjects as on the boards : this
circle turns on a pivot, and contains a
magnet. A perfon places any one of
the four boards in one of the boxes privately, and you place the other box, with
the pafteboard circle, over it ; when the
magnet in the board will turn the circle, till that part of it which is under an
opening made in the top of the box,
prefent the fame picture as that on the
board, and which is fuppofed to be
drawn by a little painter concealed in
the box.

RECRE-

RECRE-

R E C R E A T I O N XXXVI. p. 153

The myſtical dial.

There is a ſmall box, (Plate IX. Fig. 2.)
and four boards, Fig. 3 ; in each of theſe
boards a magnet is placed, in a different
poſition, and on it a different number
is wrote. A perſon is to place one of
the boards in the box, and to chooſe
whether the needle of the dial, Fig. 4,
when placed over the box, ſhall point
to the whole, the half, the double, or
triple of the number on the board; and
you then place the dial on the box in a
determinate poſition.

R E C R E A T I O N XXXVII. p. 156

The enchanted ewer.

A hollow cone is placed in a ewer, (Plate
X. Fig. 1.) at the bottom of which is a

Vol. III.   T   hole :

hole : under that hole a convex mirror, and between the hole and the mirror is a pasteboard circle, Fig. 3, that turns on a pivot. The ewer is placed on a stand, Fig. 1, in which is a drawer. The pasteboard circle is divided into four parts, in three of which are painted the same figures as on three of the boards, Fig. 5, and the fourth is left blank : this pasteboard circle contains a magnetic needle, and the four boards have each a concealed magnet ; therefore when one of them is put in the drawer under the ewer, the circle will correspond to the position of that magnet, and a person looking into the top of the ewer will see his own face surrounded with the head dress of the figure in the drawer.

RECRE—

T 2　　　　RECRE-

RECREATION XXXIX. p. 164.

The box and dice.

At one end of a long hollow cafe or pedeftal (Plate XI. Fig. 1.) is drawn a circle, divided into twenty equal parts, in
which are marked the points that can
be thrown by two dice.   At the center
of this circle is placed a magnetic needle, which is directed by a bar underneath it.   At the other end of this pedeftal is a vafe that has different divifions, in which dice are placed, that
feem to be thofe thrown in at the top of
the vafe.   When the needle is turned
round it will ftop at thofe points in
the circle that anfwer to thofe on the
dice in the vafe : the bar underneath the
circle having been previoufly fet to thofe
points.

R E-

RECREATION XL.   p. 168

The box of flowers.

There are two cafes, (Plate XI. Fig. 3 and
4) in each of which two flowers are
placed, and in each of them is concealed a magnetic bar, fixed in a certain
direction : thefe cafes are put in a box
of very thin wood, Fig. 2. and when
the magnetic perfpective is held over
them, it is readily difcovered, by the
direction of the needle, what flower is
in that part of the box.

RECREATION XLI.   p. 170

The box of metals.

At the bottom of a box, whofe cover is
as thin as poffible, (Plate XII. Fig. 1.)
are fix holes, exactly fimilar, and in thefe
holes are placed tablets, that each of
them contain a magnet, in a different
T 3 pofition,

position, and that is covered with a thin plate of different metal. There is a magnetic perspective, Fig. 2, that has two circles marked with the letters of the different metals, and from its center is drawn an index. If this perspective be held over any one of the tablets, in such manner that its index is perpendicular to the side of the box, the needle in the perspective will point to the letter of the metal over which it then is. This box of metals far preferable to those formerly exhibited, p. 173.

RECREATION XLII.   p. 174

The magnetic oracle.

There are eight tablets that each contain a magnet, in a different position; there is also a dial marked with the digits from 1 to 8, (Plate XII. Fig. 5.) and thirty-two small rundlets that have the same numbers. On the tablets questions

tions are wrote, and four of the rundlets contain different anfwers to each quef-tion. A perfon puts the dial over any one of the tablets, and turning the hand round it ftops at the number which is marked on the rundlets that contain the anfwer.

The incomprehenfible card.

A very thin fteel magnet is concealed in a card. You prefent a pack to a perfon that he may draw one, and offer the card with the magnet: he is then at liberty to conceal the card, or replace it, privately, in the pack, and you tell, by your perfpective, whether it be there or not.

The two magical cards.

At the bottom of a fmall box (Plate XII. Fig. 6.) a pivot is placed, on which

T 4 turns

turns a pasteboard circle that contains a
touched needle, and on which two cards
are painted; and in the top of the box
is a hole, by which those cards are visible.
You are to have a pack of cards that
has a long and a wide card, which are
the same as those in the box : these two
cards are to be drawn by two persons,
and by applying your magnetic wand
to the box, either of the cards becomes
visible, at pleasure.

RECREATION XLV. p. 189

The magnetic planetarium,

A round moveable pasteboard is placed at the
bottom of a box, (Pl. XIII. Fig. 1.) at its
center a circle is drawn, and seven other
circles round that ; and cross each of these
a magnet is fixed, Over this pasteboard
another is placed, on which are drawn
eight corresponding circles; in that at
the center seven questions are wrote,
and in the others are words that answer
those

thofe queftions, and on each of thefe
circles turns a magnetic needle. The
lower circle is moved by a hand fixed
to its axis, which comes through the
upper circle ; and when the lower pafteboard is moved, the attraction of its
magnets moves all the needles on the
upper board. A perfon therefore fet-
ting the hand to any one of the queftions in the central circle, the needles on
the other circles immediately point to
the words that compofe the anfwer.

CONSTRUCTION OF THE MAGNETICAL AND MECHANICAL TABLE. p. 186.

Under the top of this table, (Plate XIV.
Fig. 1.) and about one inch and a half
from it, is another furface, on which
is placed the magnetic apparatus, by
which the fubfequent recreations are
performed. The legs of this table,
Fig. 2, are hollow, and through them,
and the ftep that joins to them,
goes

goes a cord, that comes out behind
the partition, and paffing over a pulley, Plate XV, has a weight joined
to the end of it, and to it is likewife
fixed an index. On the upper furface of this table are placed, in fuccef-
ceffion, three circles, (Plate XIV. Fig.
1, 4, and 5.) on whofe circumference
are different numbers of divifions, that
correfpond to the divifions in the feveral columns of the table, Plate XV.
One of thefe circles is placed on that
part of the table which is over the magnetic bar; on the circle is placed a fhallow bafon with water, in which floats
the figure of a firen, that contains a
touched needle : therefore, when the
perfon behind the partition places the
index on the cord againft any one divifion of the table, he will, by moving
the magnetic bar under the circle, make
the firen point to a letter or number in
a correfponding divifion of that circle.

R E-

On three cards that are each of a different fize, are wrote the names of
three perfons or cities. Thefe three
cards being given to any perfon, he
keeps one of them and returns you the
other two, which you lay afide without
looking at them, and the firen immediately points to the letters that compofe
the word on the card the perfon has
taken. For you diftinguifh by the
touch which of the three cards is chofe,
and by certain words, previoufly agreed
on, make it known to the confederate.

A part of the ftep on which the operator ftands goes through the partition,
6 and

and is moveable, like a lever. The watch is laid on the table, and the operator preffes down the ftep with his foot as many times as are equal to the number of hours; which the confederate behind the partition obferving, makes the firen point to that number. A fimilar fignal is then made for the quarters and minutes.

To make the firen point to three numbers that have been chofen by three different perfons,

Thefe three numbers are drawn from a bag, in which there are feveral divifions; and the confederate knowing what thofe numbers are, makes the firen point to them.

A ques-

RECREATION XLVII. p. 200

The fagacious fwan.

On the top of an oblong box (Plate XVI. Fig. 1.) is placed a fhallow bafon, in which floats the figure of a fwan, that contains a touched needle. Round this bafon are placed fix fmall vafes, and in each of them is put an anfwer to a queftion.

tion. At the other end of the box is an ivory egg, on a hollow ftand. There are fix etwees, Fig. 3, of different lengths, and that each contain a queftion. A perfon having chofe one of the etwees, takes out the queftion, and puts the etwee into the egg, and by fhutting down the top of the egg preffes the etwee down the hollow ftand, and againft a movement in the box, Fig. 2, by which mean a magnetic bar is brought under a particular part of the bafon, according to the length of the etwee, and the fwan is thereby directed to the vafe that contains an anfwer to the queftion.

THE COMMUNICATIVE BELL. p. 205

In a hollow circular box (Plate XVII. Fig. 1.) there is fixed a fmall bell, and at the center of the box is a pivot, on which is placed a touched needle, that has at each end a fmall brafs knob. The bottom of this box is covered with gauze.

manner directed in the firſt volume, and they will then be in a determinate order; of which the confederate having a copy, and hearing the name of the card the perſon has choſe, makes the bell ſtrike the number at which it is from the top.

RECREATION XLIX.   p. 211

The magnetic balance.

A pair of ſteel ſcales, that are gilt and very true, (Plate XVII. Fig. 2.) are ſuſpended over the magnetic table, near the part under which the bar is placed. Two pieces of money that are preciſely of the ſame weight being put in theſe ſcales either of them is made to preponderate at pleaſure. The confederate, at a ſignal given, bringing the bar under one or other of the ſcales.

RECRE-

RECREATION L.   p. 214

The sympathetic dials.

One of thefe dials has a catch on the outfide, by which it is ftopped at pleafure:
the other has a fteel catch within the cafe,
that takes the fly of the movement.
A large bar in the magnetic table, when
brought under this dial, attracts the
catch and puts the wheels in motion,
but when the bar is moved from it, the
motion ceafes immediately. You therefore give the dial with the ftop to a perfon, and tell him that when he ftops that
dial, or puts it in motion, the other on
the table will, by fympathy, ftop or move
alfo; and by mounting the ftep you
make it act accordingly.

CONSTRUCTION OF THE MAGNETIC ROLLER. p. 217.

This roller confifts of a long and narrow
piece of wood, (Pl. XVII. Fig. 5.) on
which there are twelve circles, and in
each of them a magnet, placed in dif-

VOL. III.   U   ferent

ferent directions from the others. This
roller is placed at the bottom of the magnetic table, and moves upon two cylinders, being drawn by a string that goes
down a leg of the table, through the
partition, and over a pulley placed on the
other side of it : to this string a weight
and an index are fastened.   Under the
pulley is placed a table, p. 220, that has
five columns, which contain numbers,
letters, the names of cards, countries,
&c. and in each of these columns are ten
divisions that correspond to the ten circles on the roller : so that when the index on the string is set by the confederate, against any one of those divisions,
the circle on the roller that answers to it
is brought to a certain part of the magnetic table, that the bar it contains may
act on the needle of some machine to be
placed over it.

R E-

U 2   it

It has a magnetie needle for an index, which points to any one of the ten divisions on the circle, according to the position of the magnet in the part of the roller over which it is placed. Method of showing by this dial the numbers that two persons have chose, their sum, or their product, p. 226.

RECREATION LIII. p. 228

The magical game of all-fours.

There must be a circle with twelve divisions, on six of which cards are painted, and to which six of the divisions of the roller correspond. A pack of cards are previously disposed, according to the manner explained in the first volume; so that after the cards are dealt they can be played only one way. The other person plays his cards, yours remain on the table, and every time you are to play you direct another person to look in at the top of the box, (Pl. XVIII. Fig. 2.) and see what card is played, your con-

6   federate

federate having brought the proper card in view, by moving the roller.

RECREATION LIV. p. 231

The intelligent fly.

The space between two concentric circles contained in a box (Pl. XVIII. Fig. 5.) is divided into ten equal parts, in each of which a letter is wrote ; and at the center of the circle, is placed a pivot, that holds a magnetic needle, at the end of which is the figure of a fly : all the needle, except that part to which the fly is fixed, is concealed by a paper placed over it. There are laid on a table a parcel of cards, properly packed, and on each of them a question is wrote. You ask a person at what number the card shall be to which the fly shall give him an answer. When he has determined, you place the box over the roller, and your confederate knowing the question on the card, makes the fly point to the letters that compose the answer.

RECRE-

RECREATION LV. p. 236

The multifarious verfe.

On eight tablets that are of the fame fize, and that exactly fill a box, (Plate XIX. Fig. 1.) are wrote the eight words of a Latin verfe, and in each of them is placed a magnet, in a different pofition. Over this box is placed a board, Fig. 2, that has eight circles, whofe centers are directly over thofe of the tablets : round each of thefe circles are wrote the eight words of the Latin verfe, and on each of them is placed a needle. Over the board and box is placed a glafs frame, Fig. 3. If a perfon put the tablets in any pofition privately, then cover the box over with paper, and place it under the board, the needle on each circle will point to the word on the tablet under it ; fo that by looking into the top of the box you will always know in what order the tablets are placed.

R E C R E-

RECREATION LVI. p. 240.

The communicative mirror.

In a box (Plate XX. Fig. 1.) is placed a pivot, on which is fixed a pasteboard circle, Fig. 2, that has a touched needle, and on which are painted three cards. Over this pasteboard is a hole, in the top of the box, and over that is placed a hollow glass pedestal, on which is fixed a tube, containing an inclined mirror. There are three tablets that have each a card, similar to those on the circle, and a magnetic bar. One of these being placed in the box, Fig. 3, and that put in the other box, Fig. 1, under the circle, it will place itself in a corresponding position; so that a person looking into the tube will see the same card as that on the tablet concealed in the box, and he will seem to see it in the mirror placed opposite the tube.

R E-

The box of dice by reflection.

At each end of a long box (Pl. XX. Fig. 4.) is a fmall hole, and over the ends are placed two hollow cubes; under each of thefe cubes is an inclined mirror, and a fmall touched needle on a pivot. The top and two longeft fides of this box are of glafs, lined with a thin paper. There are two dice, that have concealed in each of their fides a fmall magnet: fo that when thefe dice are placed in the cubes, in any pofition, you will fee, by looking in at the hole at each end of the box, the pofition of the needle under each cube, and confequently difcover which fide of each die is next the top of the box.

THE END OF THE THIRD VOLUME.

Check Out More Titles From HardPress Classics Series In this collection we are offering thousands of classic and hard to find books. This series spans a vast array of subjects — so you are bound to find something of interest to enjoy reading and learning about.

Subjects:
Architecture
Art
Biography & Autobiography
Body, Mind &Spirit
Children & Young Adult
Dramas
Education
Fiction
History
Language Arts & Disciplines
Law
Literary Collections
Music
Poetry
Psychology
Science
…and many more.

Visit us at www.hardpress.net

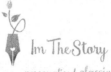

CPSIA information can be obtained
at www.ICGtesting.com
Printed in the USA
BVHW070849200819
556223BV00024B/3597/P

9 781406 972924